The Art Institute of Chicago

MUSEUM STUDIES

VOLUME 14, NO. 1

The Art Institute of Chicago Museum Studies
VOLUME 14, NO. 1

© 1988 by The Art Institute of Chicago
ISSN 0069-3235
ISBN 0-226-02813-5

Published by the Art Institute of Chicago, Michigan Avenue at Adams Street, Chicago, IL 60603.
Distributed by The University of Chicago Press, Journals Division, P.O. Box 37005, Chicago, IL
60637. Regular subscription rates: $12 for members of the Art Institute, $16 for other individuals,
and $30 for institutions. Back issues are available from The Art Institute of Chicago Museum Shop
and The University of Chicago Press. Single copies are $8.50 for individuals and $15.50 for
institutions; single-copy price for vol. 12, no. 2, is $12.95 for individuals and $19.50 for institutions.

Editor of *Museum Studies:* Susan F. Rossen; Associate Editors: Robert V. Sharp and Elizabeth A.
Pratt; Production Manager: Katherine A. Houck; Designer: Binns & Lubin, New York.

12,000 copies of volume 14, number 1, were typeset in Stempel Garamond by Trufont Typogra-
phers, Hicksville, NY, and printed on 70lb. Frostbrite Matte by American Printers and Lithog-
raphers, Chicago, IL.

Front cover: View from the north of the Roger McCormick Memorial Court within the Daniel F.
and Ada L. Rice Building of The Art Institute of Chicago, 1988. Photo: Tom Cinoman.

Back cover: View from the east of the Grand Staircase and second-floor galleries of the Allerton
Building, following their renovation in 1987. Photo: Tom Cinoman.

Photography credits: Unless otherwise indicated in the caption, all illustrations are from photographs or other works in the collections of the archives, the Ryerson and Burnham Libraries, the
Department of Architecture, or the planning office of The Art Institute of Chicago, and were
produced by the Department of Photographic Services, Alan Newman, Executive Director. All
photographs of the Rice Building are by Tom Cinoman. Wherever possible, the original photographer has been credited, regardless of the source of the photograph.

The Art Institute of Chicago Museum Studies is published through the generosity of the Sterling
Morton Charitable Trust, with additional support from the Mellon Foundation Endowment for
scholarly publishing.

The Art Institute of Chicago Museum Studies

Volume 14, No. 1

Figure 1. View from the southeast of The Art Institute of Chicago, c.1910.

Preface

*E*arly photographs of the Art Institute's 1893 building on Michigan Avenue tell us much more than what the architecture looked like. Views taken from the east record a pristine Renaissance-revival palazzo; the crisply detailed Indiana limestone reflects the early morning light with all the confidence of a classical temple secure on its acropolis. But on closer examination it is clear that this building rests not upon God-given rock but upon a rubble-strewn expanse of recent landfill. It is bordered on the west by an emerging range of commercial structures that were redefining modern architecture and on the east by the railroad tracks that converged on this barren strip of lakefront from the Atlantic and the Pacific. Together they offer a partial explanation to the question of how this brash, young city had accumulated in a brief quarter century the population, industry, wealth, and confidence to claim that it had the right to become a center of world culture.

The classically inspired forms of the 1893 building conveyed the idealism of the city's leadership more effectively than words. They spoke of a cultural institution with a sense of purpose and confidence parallel to that responsible for the more radical structures of Sullivan and Burnham, who were inventing a new vertical architecture for the modern commercial city. The Art Institute's new building gave reality to its ambition, but at the outset it was filled with plaster casts and reproductions of originals that were the pride of other cities. It was less a credible museum than an expression of the confidence that the city's new private wealth would collect the masterpieces that Chicago must acquire if its cultural claims were to be taken seriously. As with so many American museums, architecture preceded the collections it was built to house. The building was first and foremost an expression of the belief that architecture could affect social change by symbolizing and focusing the city's cultural ambitions.

The buildings that house a civic institution, even more than those serving other functions, are a fundamental indicator of its health, purpose, and role within the community it serves. The publication of this issue of *Museum Studies* reflects the importance we put on architecture in symbolizing the Art Institute's purpose and assuring its success. The chronology and essays that follow record nearly 100 years of continuous planning and building, and they present the difficult and at times controversial history of this particular institution's maturation from promise to fulfillment, from the claims of a distinguished work of architecture waiting for the contents to validate its purpose, to the present structure filled with world-renowned collections that demanded an expanded space, and an architecture both worthy of its contents and suited to the vastly extended goals that motivate the Art Institute today.

To meet the demands that nearly a century of collecting had put on a museum that had expanded only intermittently in the twentieth century, and never with the scale or ambition of the original building, it was decided in 1981 that a major addition to the Art Institute was needed. At that time a concerted effort was

Institution stems from the inspiration to live. This inspiration remains meekly expressed in our institutions today. The three great inspirations are the inspiration to learn, the inspiration to meet, and the inspiration for well-being. They all serve, really, the will to be, to express. . . .

Today . . . all of our institutions are on trial.

I believe this is so because institutions have lost the inspirations of their beginnings. The constant play of circumstances, from moment to moment unpredictable, distorts the inspired beginnings of natural agreement. The institution will die when its inspirations are no longer felt, and it operates as a matter of course. Human agreement, however, once it presents itself as a Realization, is indestructible.

LOUIS I. KAHN
Untitled lecture, 1973

5

made to understand and evaluate our architectural history with the hope that this would provide a context for intelligent future growth. That effort contributed to both the final form and style of the newly completed Daniel F. and Ada L. Rice Building and to this publication. Between 1893 and 1988, the Art Institute has come full circle from the original Shepley, Rutan and Coolidge Beaux-Arts building to Hammond, Beeby and Babka's classical-revival addition. The history of what was proposed and what was actually built between these two major building programs is essential to our understanding of the museum as it exists today.

This story is also an important chapter in the history of American museum architecture and the struggle between classicism and modernism which has been one of its underlying themes. The Art Institute's architecture demonstrates that struggle more clearly than does any other museum. An obvious irony is that the idealism of the 1890s in Chicago resulted in a classicizing structure in the very city that was pioneering modernism. By the 1930s and the Century of Progress Exposition, a utopian confidence in the future, frequently at the expense of the past, had led to the rejection of the Beaux-Arts tradition, but the Art Institute's ambitious projects of this period remained mostly unbuilt. When a full-fledged modernist building was finally realized with Walter Netsch's 1974–77 addition, it was primarily dedicated to housing the School of the Art Institute and not the museum. By the 1980s, when the Institute was again prepared to undertake major expansion, the historical moment had changed again, to the point where an addition that is frankly classicizing could, without apology, be both a strong contemporary statement and a successful solution to the collection's needs, as well as a reinforcement of the institution's historic identity.

While today's culture is clearly characterized by doubt and pragmatism in contrast to the confidence of the 1890s, the Rice Building is more properly called classical revival than postmodern. Its ornamentation is not externally applied, and there is no hint of the irony that saps the integrity of so many recent museum buildings. The ancestors of today's Art Institute, both the 1893 and 1988 designs, are Italian. They combine civic scale and importance with modest and welcoming size. They succeed in making us comfortable as individuals in a monumental context that gives added importance and seriousness to the works of art on exhibition. They achieve what Robert Venturi terms "a truly Italian delight."

Kurt Forster takes Venturi's analogy one step further in his discussion of the plan and architecture of Sabbioneta, a tiny town in the Po Valley which provides an intact example of sixteenth-century Italian thought and architecture: "Sabbioneta gives body to an idea, an image born of the past, but not realized in archaic terms. Its utopian character stems precisely from the continuous desire to project a future from the past, to conceive of the present as an ambigious mediation between the two." It is our hope that the new Rice Building, in the context of the previous architecture of the Art Institute, will demonstrate that today's museum can move beyond a strict adherence to modernism without sacrificing idealistic, or even utopian, aspirations.

JAMES N. WOOD, *Director*

The Art Institute of Chicago Buildings 1879–1988:

A Chronology

The opening of the new Rice Building in 1988 marks the completion of more than a century of growth for The Art Institute of Chicago. Over the years, additions to the original 1893 building have branched north, south, and east. New space has been excavated beneath the building and added above existing stories. Additions have bridged the tracks and enclosed existing inner spaces. In the following historical summary of the museum's physical expansion, the dates given are generally the years in which the projects were opened or unveiled to the public. Where a source of funding is not indicated, costs were generally underwritten either by the operating budget or by private subscription of members of the Board of Trustees.

This chronology was originally prepared for the 1979 Centennial Year Annual Report of The Art Institute of Chicago. It was compiled and researched by Jane Clarke, Associate Director of Museum Education, with the assistance of Louise Lutz and Linda Stark. It has been updated for this issue of *Museum Studies* by Jane Clarke and John Zukowsky, Curator of Architecture, with the assistance of John Smith, Archivist. Unless otherwise noted, all the architects and firms listed below were or are Chicago based.

FIGURE 1. Perspective rendering of a commercial building initially leased and later purchased by The Art Institute of Chicago on Michigan Avenue at Van Buren Street, 1882. Architect unknown. Photo: P. Gilbert and C. Bryson, *Chicago and Its Makers* (Chicago, 1929), p. 169.

1879

The Chicago Academy of Fine Arts is incorporated under a charter from the State of Illinois May 24 and occupies quarters in rented rooms at the southwest corner of State and Monroe streets.

1882

The name is changed to The Art Institute of Chicago, and property is leased and later purchased at the southwest corner of Michigan Avenue and Van Buren Street. The museum moves into a commercial building on the Michigan Avenue side (fig. 1). A brick addition, containing exhibition galleries and school rooms, is built fronting on Van Buren; it opens January 13, 1883. Architects: Burnham and Root.

1887

A new building on the same site opens November 19 (fig. 4). Architects: Burnham and Root.

1893

A new building at Michigan Avenue and Adams Street is planned in cooperation with the World's Columbian Exposition. The Chicago Park District Board allots the land; the Fair Corporation contributes $200,000; and the Art Institute supplies $265,000 from the sale of its former building to the Chicago Club and raises $120,000 through public subscription. The building is occupied by the World's Congress Auxiliary of the World's Columbian Exposition from May 1 through October 31. Members inspect the building May 12. The Art Institute takes possession November 1, and the building formally opens with Members' reception December 8. Architects: Shepley, Rutan and Coolidge, Boston, Massachusetts. (See Phipps, pp. 28–45.)

▷ FIGURE 2. William M. R. French (1843–1914), the first director of the Art Institute, from 1879 to 1914.

▽ FIGURE 3. Charles L. Hutchinson (1854–1924), the first president of the Art Institute's Board of Trustees, from 1882 until his death. Photo: Chicago Historical Society.

▽ FIGURE 4. View of the second Art Institute building (at right; now demolished), c. 1887, adjacent to the Studebaker (now Fine Arts) Building and the Auditorium Building.

FIGURE 5. Charles Coolidge (1858–1936) of the architectural firm of Shepley, Rutan and Coolidge. Photo: Shepley Bulfinch Richardson and Abbott, architects, Boston.

FIGURE 6. Fullerton Hall as built in 1898. The stained-glass dome and crystal chandelier (now lost) were designed by Louis Comfort Tiffany (1848–1933).

FIGURE 7. Ryerson Library, built in 1901.

1903

Blackstone Hall is added adjacent to the east wall of the original building, creating a ground-level gallery two stories high for the display of architectural and sculptural casts (fig. 10). Architects: Shepley, Rutan and Coolidge. Funding: Gift of Mr. and Mrs. Timothy B. Blackstone.

1907

An east-west bridge is added across Blackstone Hall at the main-floor level; a gallery adjacent to Ryerson Library stacks is added for the Department of Prints and Drawings. Architects: Shepley, Rutan and Coolidge. Funding: Subscription from trustees and other donors.

1909

Second-floor galleries running north and south above Blackstone Hall, parallel to Illinois Central Railroad tracks, are completed; five galleries open October 19, 1909; three galleries open January 4, 1910. Architects: Shepley, Rutan and Coolidge.

1909/10

A balustrade and terrace are added on the north, south, and west sides of the building in conjunction with the widening of Michigan Avenue, and the lions are moved back twelve feet (see fig. 13). Architects: Shepley, Rutan and Coolidge.

△ FIGURE 8. View from the north of the Michigan Avenue lobby, c. 1901–10. At left is the foot of the original staircase to the second-floor galleries, and the entrance to Ryerson Library. At center is a gallery of plaster casts of antique sculpture, in the space now occupied by the Museum Shop (see also fig. 17). The balcony opening above is no longer extant.

▷ FIGURE 9. View from the north of the second-floor galleries, c. 1901–10. At left is the top of the original staircase and the windows that looked east onto an area later filled by the Grand Staircase.

▷ FIGURE 10. View from the south of Blackstone Hall, c. 1905.

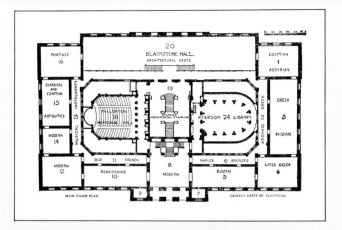

△ FIGURE 11. Plan of the first-floor galleries, 1905. The first-floor galleries were mainly for the display of sculpture and plaster casts, while those of the second-floor were intended for paintings. Photo: *Bulletin of The Art Institute of Chicago*, 1905.

▽ FIGURE 12. Plan of the second-floor galleries, 1907. Note that the Grand Staircase has not yet been built. ·Photo: *Bulletin of The Art Institute of Chicago*, 1907.

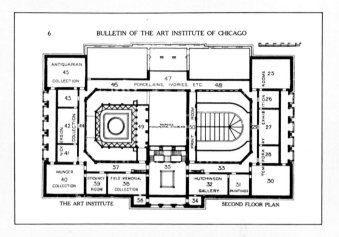

▽ FIGURE 13. View from the southwest of the Art Institute and Michigan Avenue, c. 1910, following the addition of the balustrade and terrace.

FIGURE 14. View from the northeast of the Art Institute, c. 1910. Blackstone Hall was on the first floor and painting galleries were on the second floor behind the new east facade of the museum.

FIGURE 15. View from the west of the Grand Staircase, c. 1910.

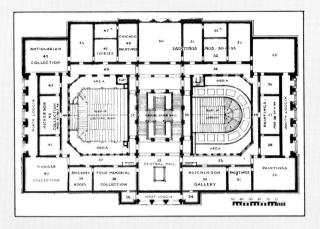

FIGURE 16. Plan of the second-floor galleries, 1910, following the erection of the Grand Staircase and the completion of galleries above Blackstone Hall. Photo: *Bulletin of The Art Institute of Chicago*, 1910.

FIGURE 17. View from the north of the first-floor gallery south of the Michigan Avenue lobby, c. 1910 (see also fig. 8).

1910

The Grand Staircase is completed; work continues intermittently on the architectural ornament of the gallery around the stairs (never completed); work will finally cease in 1929 (fig. 15). The original plans called for a great dome over the staircase (see Phipps, pp. 28–45). No funds for this dome are ever found.

1911

An administration building is completed to the north of the main building. Architects: Shepley, Rutan and Coolidge. To be demolished about 1958 during the construction of the Ferguson Building (see Bruegmann, pp. 57–81).

13

1913

Fountain of the Great Lakes, a bronze sculpture by Lorado Taft, is dedicated in its location on the south lawn adjacent to the terrace (fig. 18). Commissioned in 1907, it is the first gift of the B. F. Ferguson Monument Fund, established in 1905 by Ferguson's will, which named the trustees of the Art Institute as trustees of the fund. To be moved at time of the construction of Morton Wing (1962). Architects of the base: Shepley, Rutan and Coolidge.

1916

A two-story bridge addition (Gunsaulus Hall) spans the Illinois Central tracks (figs. 19, 20). Architects: Shepley, Rutan and Coolidge; Coolidge and Hodgdon. Funding: First-floor gallery gift of William H. Miner in honor of Dr. Frank W. Gunsaulus.

A shipping room is constructed in the sub-basement of the 1911 administrative building. It will be either demolished or incorporated in the construction of the Ferguson Building (1958).

1917

George Washington, a bronze replica of the sculpture made by Jean Antoine Houdon for the State Capitol building in Richmond, Virginia, is placed at the Michigan Avenue entrance. Funding: Purchased through the B.F. Ferguson Monument Fund.

FIGURE 18. Lorado Taft (1860–1936), *Fountain of the Great Lakes*, 1907–13. The fountain is seen just after its installation in 1913 in its original location adjacent to the south terrace of the museum.

△
FIGURE 19. West entrance to
Gunsaulus Hall, c. 1916–20.

◁ FIGURE 20. View from
the north of the Gunsaulus
Hall addition, c. 1920. The
1911 administration building
is visible in the right fore-
ground.

▽ FIGURE 21. Aerial view
from the southwest of the
Art Institute's Allerton
Building, Gunsaulus Hall,
and the Goodman Theatre
(upper right), c. 1925–30.

1920

The Burnham Library of Architecture, constructed south of and adjacent to the Ryerson Library, opens on January 12 (fig. 22). Architect: Howard Van Doren Shaw. Funding: Bequest of Daniel H. Burnham.

1924

The Hutchinson Wing galleries are added east of the Illinois Central Railroad tracks. Architects: Coolidge and Hodgdon. Funding: Contributions to the Hutchinson Wing Fund in memory of Charles L. Hutchinson, the Art Institute's president from 1882 to 1924.

The George Alexander McKinlock, Jr., Memorial Court is landscaped (fig. 23). Architects: Coolidge and Hodgdon. Funding: Gift of Mr. and Mrs. George A. McKinlock in memory of their son who died in World War I.

1925

The Kenneth Sawyer Goodman Memorial Theatre (683 seats) is built (see figs. 21, 24). Architect: Howard Van Doren Shaw. Funding: Gift of William O. and Erna Sawyer Goodman in memory of their son who died in World War I.

1926

The Mather addition on the ground level of the central building creates space for a new paint shop, photography studio, storage, Members' Room, restaurant, and tea room. Architects: Holabird and Roche. Funding: Gift of Alonzo C. Mather.

FIGURE 22. View from the east of the new Burnham Library of Architecture, c. 1920. The doors at right led to the present reading room of the combined Ryerson and Burnham Libraries.

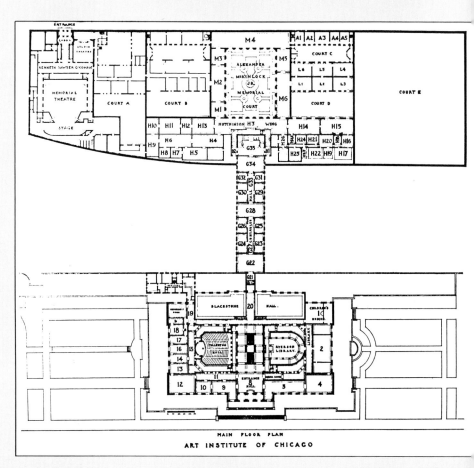

MAIN FLOOR PLAN
ART INSTITUTE OF CHICAGO

FIGURE 23. The George Alexander McKinlock, Jr., Memorial Court was landscaped in 1924. Photo: *Bulletin of The Art Institute of Chicago* 18, 7 (Oct. 1924), p. 92.

◁ FIGURE 24. Plan of the first and second floors of the Art Institute, c. 1930.

▽ FIGURE 25. View from the southeast of McKinlock Court after remodeling and installation of *Fountain of the Tritons* by Carl Milles (1875–1955), c. 1931.

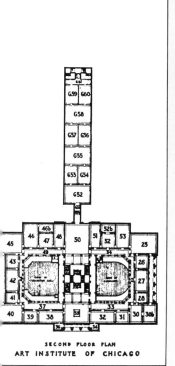

SECOND FLOOR PLAN
ART INSTITUTE OF CHICAGO

1927

The Agnes W. Allerton Wing is added for the Department of Textiles (galleries south of Hutchinson Wing; see fig. 24). Architects: Coolidge and Hodgdon. Funding: Gift of Robert Allerton in memory of his mother.

An addition to the School links Goodman Theatre and McKinlock Court (see fig. 24).

1929

The Studio Theatre is added to the Goodman Theatre (see fig. 24). Architect: Howard Van Doren Shaw.

The Burnham Library of Architecture space is turned over to the Ryerson Library, and the Burnham Library is relocated in adjacent galleries south of Ryerson Library. Architects: Hubert Burnham, William J. Smith, and Earl A. Reed, Jr. Funding: Gifts of Walter Brewster, Alfred Hamill, Frank Logan, and the D. H. Burnham family.

1931

Fountain of the Tritons, a sculpture by Carl Milles, is installed in McKinlock Court (fig. 25). Architects: Holabird and Root. Funding: Gift of twelve Swedish citizens of Chicago.

1938

Goodman Theatre adds space for offices, work shops, and scenery storage. Architects: Holabird and Root.

1939

The Robert Allerton Wing is added (galleries to the south of Hutchinson Wing, and two inner courts). Architects: Holabird and Root. Funding: Gift of Robert Allerton.

1940–53

World War II and shortages of materials following the war permit only basic maintenance of structure.

1954

Interior reconstruction creates space for the first Art Rental and Sales Gallery on the main floor. Funding: In part by the Woman's Board.

1958

Blackstone Hall is reconstructed to create main-floor Oriental galleries, study area, and storage. Architects: Holabird and Root. Funding: Emergency Fund Campaign.

The B. F. Ferguson Memorial Building (west of the Illinois Central Railroad tracks and north of the central building) is constructed for administrative and curatorial offices, museum education, conservation, museum photography, shipping room, carpentry and paint shops; this releases spaces in existing buildings for gallery use (fig. 26). Architects: Holabird and Root and Burgee. Funding: Life Membership Fund Principal and B. F. Ferguson Monument Fund Income. (See Bruegmann, pp. 57–81.)

1959

Ground-level reconstruction of the Blackstone Hall area provides for the Preston Owsley Morton Auditorium (120 seats) (gift of Mrs. Sterling Morton); the Lacy Armour Gallery, adjacent to Morton Auditorium (gift of Mrs. Laurance H. Armour); and a cafeteria and dining rooms. Architects: Holabird and Root.

Remodeling of the main floor provides the first Glore Print Study Room. Architect: Daniel Brenner. Funding: Gift of Mrs. Charles F. Glore in memory of her husband.

18

FIGURE 26. View from the northwest of the B. F. Ferguson Memorial Building (1958) and the north Stanley McCormick Memorial Court (1960), c. 1960.

FIGURE 27. Progress chart of new construction and remodeling, including the new Ferguson Building of the Art Institute, 1958–59. Photo: *Bulletin of The Art Institute of Chicago* 53, 3 (Oct. 1959), pp. 20–21.

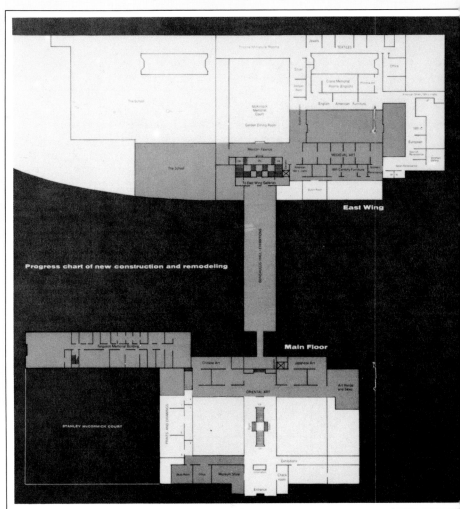

▷ FIGURES 28, 29. *Right*, John A. Holabird (1886–1945) and *below*, John W. Root, Jr. (1887–1963). The firm of Holabird and Root and Burgee designed the Ferguson Building (1958) and the north McCormick Court (1960).

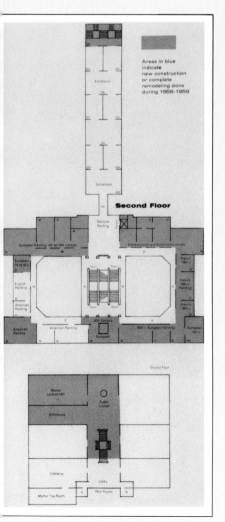

Areas in blue indicate new construction or complete remodeling done during 1958-1959

Second Floor

1960

Interior ground-level construction provides a new Members' Room and the first Woman's Board Room. Architect: Daniel Brenner. Funding: Gift of the Woman's Board.

The northern of the two existing inner garden courts (adjacent to the textile galleries) is landscaped. To be demolished in 1986 for construction of the Rice Building. Landscape architects: Simonds, West, and Blair/Clauss Bros. Funding: Gift of the Kenilworth Garden Club.

The Stanley McCormick Memorial Court, the north garden at Michigan Avenue and Monroe Street, is constructed (see fig. 26). Architects: Holabird and Root and Burgee. Funding: Gift of Mrs. Stanley McCormick in memory of her husband. (See Bruegmann, pp. 57–81.)

1961

A building for the School is completed east of the Illinois Central Railroad tracks. Architects: Shaw, Metz and Associates.

1962

Three flag poles are installed on the north terrace adjacent to the Stanley McCormick Memorial Court. Designers: Shaw, Metz and Associates. Funding: Gift of Mrs. Stanley McCormick in memory of her husband.

The Morton Wing (south of the central building, balancing the Ferguson Building to the north) is added to provide a large, main-floor exhibition area and galleries on the second floor (fig. 30). Architects: Shaw, Metz and Associates. Gift of Sterling and Preston Owsley Morton. (See Bruegmann, pp. 57–81.)

1962

Ground-level remodeling in the central building creates an expanded Art Rental and Sales Gallery between the Lacy Armour Gallery and the Members' Room. Funding: In part by the Woman's Board through gifts from the Art Rental and Sales Gallery.

1964

Reconstruction of the ground-level space in the central building creates the Junior Museum, planned and financed by the Woman's Board in cooperation with the Junior League of Chicago, Inc. Architect: Arthur W. Myrhum.

1965

The Stanley McCormick Memorial Court, the south garden at Michigan Avenue and Jackson Boulevard, is constructed and the *Fountain of the Great Lakes* is reinstalled against the west wall of the Morton Wing (see fig. 30). Gift of Mrs. Stanley McCormick in memory of her husband. Landscape architect: Dan Kiley. (See Bruegmann, pp. 57–81.)

1967

Reconstruction projects provide new exhibition space, the A. Montgomery Ward Gallery (south of Ryerson Library), renovation of the Ryerson and Burnham Libraries, and creation of the Burnham Library of Architecture gallery, a semicircular space overlooking the reading room of the Ryerson Library. Architects: C. F. Murphy Associates and Brenner, Danforth and Rockwell. Funding: Underwritten by many generous donors and foundations.

1968

The original central building is named the Robert Allerton Building, in recognition of the devotion and generosity of Robert Allerton, honorary president and a long-time trustee.

FIGURE 30. *Above, left*, view from the west of the Morton Wing (1962) and the south Stanley McCormick Memorial Court (1965).

FIGURE 31. *Above, right*, Alfred Shaw (1895–1970) of Shaw, Metz and Associates, architects of the Morton Wing.

▽ FIGURE 32. Aerial view from the east of the Art Institute's East Wing and School of the Art Institute under construction, c. 1974–76. Photo: Tigerhill Studio.

△ FIGURE 33. View from the northeast of the East Garden of the Art Institute and the Columbus Drive entrance to the Arthur Rubloff Building.

▽ FIGURE 34. Walter Netsch (born 1920) of Skidmore, Owings and Merrill, architects of the East Wing and School. Photo: Stuart-Rodgers.

1973
Reconstruction of the Department of Prints and Drawings provides galleries, offices, conservation area, storage, and remodeled Glore Print Study Room. Architects: Skidmore, Owings and Merrill. Funding: Gift of Mrs. Joseph Regenstein; bequest of Mrs. Tiffany Blake.

1974
Ground is broken May 3 along Columbus Drive for facilities that will provide the School with a unified space; a new east entry to the museum; an auditorium; new galleries; and a new cafeteria, dining room, and Members' Lounge (see figs. 32, 33). Architects: Skidmore, Owings and Merrill; Walter Netsch, project designer. Funding: Gifts of individuals, corporations, and foundations to the Centennial Fund. Unless otherwise indicated, the projects completed through 1978 were all funded by the Centennial Fund and the architects were Skidmore, Owings and Merrill; Walter Netsch, project designer. (See Bruegmann, pp. 57–81.)

The McKinlock Court upper-level gallery space (formerly a terrace) is completed and temporarily occupied by the School, pending the completion of new School facilities.

The southern of the two existing inner garden courts (adjacent to the textile galleries) is named the Roger McCormick Memorial Court. To be demolished in 1986 for construction of the Rice Building; the name will be transferred to the sculpture court of the new building.

1976
New School facilities are dedicated October 6 (see Bruegmann, pp. 57–81).

21

1976

Celebration of the 200th Anniversary of the Founding of the Republic, a sculpture in granite and steel by Isamu Noguchi, is dedicated November 30 in front of the Columbus Drive building. Supervising architects for the installation: Skidmore, Owings and Merrill. Funding: Commissioned by the trustees of the B. F. Ferguson Monument Fund.

1977

The reconstructed Trading Room and entrance arch from the Chicago Stock Exchange Building (Adler and Sullivan, 1893–94; demolished 1972), are dedicated April 6: the Trading Room is adjacent to the Columbus Drive entrance (fig. 35); the arch is in the East Garden (fig. 36). Architects: Vinci-Kenny Architects. Funding: Gift of the Walter E. Heller Foundation and its president, Mrs. Edwin J. De Costa; additional gifts made by the City of Chicago, Mrs. Eugene A. Davidson, the Graham Foundation for Advanced Studies in the Fine Arts, and Three Oaks Wrecking Company.

The Columbus Drive Entrance, restaurants, Members' Lounge, Columbus Drive Auditorium (950 seats), and other facilities are completed in the Columbus Drive building. Members' opening is held April 7.

The East Garden between Monroe Street and Jackson Boulevard, facing Columbus Drive, is dedicated. Landscape architects: Skidmore, Owings and Merrill; project director, George Dickey. Funding: Gift of the Centennial Fund and numerous donors in memory of Walter S. Frazier.

FIGURE 35. View of the reconstructed Trading Room from the Chicago Stock Exchange, 1976–77.

FIGURE 36. The Chicago Stock Exchange entrance arch was installed in the Art Institute's East Garden in 1977.

Stained-glass *America Windows*, designed by Marc Chagall to commemorate America's Bicentennial, in memory of Mayor Richard J. Daley, are installed in the west wall of the upper-level McKinlock Court galleries. Dedication ceremonies are held May 15. Funding: Gift of the City of Chicago, the Auxiliary Board, and Mr. and Mrs. William Wood Prince.

The new Woman's Board Room, relocated in lower-level McKinlock Court space, opens September 6. Vacated spaces become museum offices.

Reconstructed Department of Textiles, including galleries, offices, study room, and conservation and storage facilities, opens December 13. Funding: Gifts of Mrs. Julian Armstrong, Jr., and Mr. Edwin A. Seipp, Jr., in memory of their parents, Mr. and Mrs. Edwin A. Seipp, and Mr. and Mrs. John V. Farwell III; the Grace R. Smith Textile Fund; and the Centennial Fund.

1978
The upper- and lower-level McKinlock Court galleries are reinstalled as exhibition galleries following their temporary use by the School.

1982
Ground-floor reconstruction creates galleries, study room, storage vaults, conservation laboratory, and offices for the Department of Photography. Architects: Skidmore, Owings and Merrill. Funding: Gifts of Mr. and Mrs. Leigh B. Block, the Woods Charitable Trust, the Kresge Foundation, the Robert R. McCormick Foundation, and many individual donors.

1983

Large Interior Form, a bronze sculpture by Henry Moore, is unveiled in the north Stanley McCormick Memorial Court May 6. Funding: Gift of the artist.

1985

The Department of Africa, Oceania, and the Americas galleries are relocated and reconstructed in the Allerton Building. The Columbus Drive Building and its auditorium are renamed in honor of Arthur Rubloff, in recognition of his generous gift to the Capital Campaign.

1985–87

The renovation of the Allerton Building's second-floor galleries and Grand Staircase, restoration of the interior-ring galleries, replacement of the skylight roof and laylights, and complete reinstallation of the European painting and sculpture collection, plus installation of prints and drawings in the interior-ring galleries, close large portions of the museum (see figs. 37, 38). Architects: Skidmore, Owings and Merrill. Funding: Many generous donors to the Capital Campaign, and a grant from the Pritzker family.

◁ FIGURE 37. View from the west of
the renovated Grand Staircase of the Art
Institute, 1987.

▽ FIGURE 38. The renovated and reinstalled galleries of European art now
display paintings, sculpture, prints, and
drawings together.

1987

The Michigan Avenue Entrance Lobby is restored (fig. 39); "Fragments of Chicago's Past" is installed in the second-floor gallery ringing the Grand Staircase. Architect: Office of John Vinci. Funding: Capital Campaign projects.

The completion of this two-year program of renovation and restoration is celebrated with a grand opening and free admission to the public from May 10 to May 17, 1987.

1985–88

The Daniel F. and Ada L. Rice Building is constructed (figs. 41, 42). It will add thirty-two percent more gallery space and will house the collections of American arts, European decorative arts and sculpture, and twentieth-century American art, as well as provide a large, special-exhibition space named Regenstein Hall. Architects: Hammond, Beeby and Babka. Funding: Gifts of the Rice Foundation, the Regenstein Fund, and the families of Marshall Field and Roger McCormick; the Robert R. McComick Charitable Trust; and the proceeds of a bond issue of the Chicago Park District. (See Klawans, pp. 83–98.)

The grounds facing Jackson Boulevard are landscaped. Design: Staff of the Art Institute in consultation with Richard Bumstead, University of Chicago planner.

FIGURE 39. View of the Michigan Avenue entrance lobby following its renovation in 1987.

FIGURE 40. Thomas Beeby (born 1941) of Hammond, Beeby and Babka, architects of the Daniel F. and Ada L. Rice Building.

FIGURE 41. View from the west of the Art Institute's new addition, the Daniel F. and Ada L. Rice Building, 1988.

FIGURE 42. View from the north of the Roger McCormick Memorial Court within the Rice Building.

1988
The Champlain Building (Holabird and Roche, 1903) at the corner of Wabash and Monroe streets, is purchased to consolidate off-campus School programs in one building in close proximity to the museum and the Columbus Drive facility of the School.

The Rice Building is opened, with Member Preview Days held September 9 to 16, for both the new building and the inaugural exhibition "The Art of Paul Gauguin" in Regenstein Hall. The public opening of the building and the exhibition is held September 17.

The 1893 Art Institute Building
and the "Paris of America":
Aspirations of Patrons and Architects in
Late Nineteenth-Century Chicago

LINDA S. PHIPPS, *Harvard University*

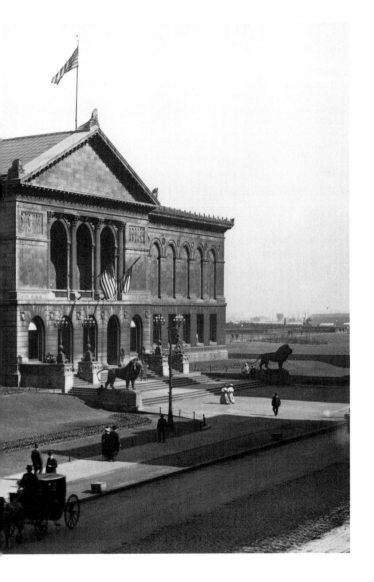

FIGURE 1. Shepley, Rutan and Coolidge, architects. The Art Institute of Chicago, 1891–93. This original structure is now called the Robert Allerton Building. Photo c. 1900.

The streets and boulevards will be improved, the great parks of the city will be made still more attractive . . . places of popular entertainment will be multiplied . . . the air will be freed from the smoke contaminations, and the great place of summer resort, with the World's Fair enhanced by all the native charms of the city and the delights of its climate, will be the Paris of America, and such it will remain. Those who . . . shall be fortunate enough to see [Chicago] in the spring of 1893 will not know it.

T he *Chicago Tribune* made this bold prediction on October 12, 1890. At the time, Chicago was known for tall, smoke-blackened office buildings; a considerable volume of trade; large, noxious stockyards; and little more. Fortunately, a league of businessmen, who owed their wealth to the city's commercial institutions, strove to improve the appearance and quality of life in their city and were determined to realize the *Tribune*'s goal. The present-day Allerton Building of The Art Institute of Chicago (1891–93; fig. 1) attests to their efforts to transform Chicago into a cultural center of international stature through the agency of the World's Columbian Exposition. For the Art Institute's Board of

Trustees, the erection of this monumental building in what they called the Italian Renaissance manner signaled Chicago's arrival among the great cities of the world and established early precedents of architectural style and building type that would greatly influence subsequent public architecture in Chicago.

On April 25, 1890, President Benjamin Harrison had signed the congressional bill awarding the World's Columbian Exposition to Chicago over New York, St. Louis, and a number of other rival cities. Chicago won the Fair partly because local businessmen had raised $5,000,000 in subscriptions to support it and the Common Council of Chicago had matched that sum. While the potential business to be generated by a successful international exposition in their home city was undoubtedly a factor underlying the subscribers' generosity, a second, more important, factor was involved. The promoters of the Fair realized that despite the great success of Chicago businesses since the devastating Fire of 1871, the city was still considered a provincial backwater. For example, the lakefront strip east of Michigan Avenue called Lake Park (now Grant Park) was unimproved marshland, enlarged by the unceremonious dumping of debris from the 1871 Fire. Instead of providing a beautiful promenade along the lake, the area embarrassed local businessmen: shanties and sheds were scattered haphazardly there, and the engines of the Illinois Central Railroad chugged along on trestles next to the shore, billowing black smoke. But, in the charged atmosphere surrounding the planning for the Fair, several civic improvement schemes were proposed, and the possibility of permanent improvements to the city became a major consideration. Central to the debate concerning the site of the Exposition was the issue of what structures might remain after it closed. The prospect of obtaining new civic buildings at little or no expense to the city compelled several special interest groups to fight vigorously over the proposed location of the Exposition. Many local businessmen who considered the squalor of the lakefront a reflection upon themselves supported the use of Lake Park, hoping to create enough land for the exhibits by filling the lake past the shoreline. By the fall of 1890, however, the prohibitive expense of filling the harbor adjacent to Lake Park forced the Exposition's directorate to decide upon a dual site, with most of the exhibits to be located in Jackson Park on the south side.[1]

Nonetheless, the Lake Park faction had not been completely defeated, as some of the buildings were still to be erected there, most notably the Palace of Fine Arts, which was intended eventually to house the Art Institute. The *Chicago Tribune* confirmed the popularity of this position:

The Art Building should be constructed carefully and well . . . when the Fair is over this great building, *so centrally located*—near the point where all the street-car systems unite, and accessible by rail as well—can be made available for city uses. A half of it would hold all the works of art Chicago would possess for many years [emphasis added].[2]

The Art Institute's trustees, many of whom served as directors of the Exposition, actively supported the Lake Park site because they saw the central location essential to the goal of their institution of reaching the greatest number of people.

The Art Institute of Chicago had been incorporated on May 24, 1879, for the purpose of maintaining a museum and a school of art. Charles L. Hutchinson, president of the Corn Exchange National Bank, was elected the first president of the Art Institute's Board of Trustees in 1882, and he served until his death in 1924. Hutchinson belonged to nearly every charitable or cultural institution in the city, and he was on the boards of several of them. Under Hutchinson's direction, the Art Institute grew steadily. Also in 1882, the Art Institute erected a modest brick addition on Van Buren Street to the rear of a commercial structure it already occupied fronting on Michigan Avenue (see Chronology, p. 7, fig. 1). By 1885, the thriving institution required a second building, begun that year and completed in November 1887 (see Chronology, p. 8, fig. 4). Grander than the first building, the second one was a handsome stone structure facing Michigan Avenue designed in the Romanesque Revival style popular at the time.[3] Both of these buildings were designed by the Chicago firm of Burnham and Root. Within three years, however, the Art Institute trustees, already forced to rent additional space in an adjacent building, were considering ways to expand their facilities once more.

Most of the trustees belonged to one or more of Chicago's men's clubs, where business decisions were often made informally, in an atmosphere of camaraderie. Like Hutchinson, they also belonged to several charitable or philanthropic organizations, and many served on the boards of other Chicago cultural institutions. The Commercial Club of Chicago, founded in 1877 "for the purpose of advancing by social intercourse and by a friendly exchange of views the prosperity and growth of the city of Chicago," served as a forum for the philanthropic activities of Hutchinson and his peers.[4]

At their monthly dinner meeting on October 25, 1890, the members of the Commercial Club, sixty of Chicago's most successful businessmen, considered the questions: "Has Chicago not reached that period when special attention should be given to the founding of art galleries and museums? Will the World's Columbian Exposition be of any benefit to this city in that direction?"[5] The list of speakers who addressed these concerns suggests that many of the arrangements between the organizations necessary for a new Art Institute building had already been made. Included were Hutchinson, who was also a director and guarantor of the Exposition and a Commercial Club member; William M. R. French, director of the Art Institute; Nathaniel K. Fairbank, an Art Institute trustee and Commercial Club member; Franklin MacVeagh, a governing member of the Art Institute and member of the Commercial Club; Thomas B. Bryan, vice-president of the Exposition directorate and a governing member of the Art Institute; and Edward T. Jeffrey, a member of the Exposition directorate and an Art Institute annual member.

As a result of the meeting, the Commercial Club appointed a committee of six members to represent it in conferring with the Exposition directorate about the "proposed memorial art museum building on the Lake Front."[6] All of the men on this committee were governing members of the Art Institute, and one was a trustee.[7] On October 31, 1890, the Art Institute trustees unanimously decided to allow Hutchinson to appoint two other trustees to assist him in his negotiations for the proposed new building. Hutchinson chose vice-president Edson Keith and Charles D. Hamill of the trustees' executive committee. Meanwhile, the Exposition directorate appointed Potter Palmer, Harlow N. Higinbotham, and Eugene S. Pike—all of whom were governing members of the Art Institute and important local businessmen—to negotiate with the Art Institute and the Commercial Club.

By December, the three committees agreed that the Exposition directors would give the Art Institute $500,000 toward the erection of a building that would house the Exposition's art department, provided that an additional $400,000 was raised through the combined efforts of the Art Institute and the Commercial Club. Yet, because its efforts duplicated those of the Art Institute, and because it generally restricted its activities to serving as a forum for ideas rather than as a fundraising organization, the Commercial Club declined. In the absence of the club's contribution, the Art Institute was to be responsible for only an additional $300,000. Optimistic at the prospect of a new building worth $800,000, the trustees called once again upon Burnham and Root for designs.

Daniel H. Burnham (1846–1912) and John Wellborn Root (1850–1891) had been preoccupied since April with plans for the Exposition grounds, and Root had been preparing designs for the Palace of Fine Arts/Art Institute building since August. In September, Burnham and Root were appointed consulting architects of the Exposition. Although other architects had developed plans for the Exposition grounds and various buildings, they were not as successful as Burnham and Root in gaining the attention of the Exposition's directorate. Solon S. Beman (1853–1914), a successful Chicago architect, had conceived plans for a Lake Park Exposition site that would include a Palace of Fine Arts. Beman's suggestion, as it was published in the *Chicago Evening Mail*, included an elaborate plan with classical landscaping and large buildings with generalized classical details. The Palace of Fine Arts, with a dome and a large arched entrance, appears in the center of the drawing.[8] Although Hutchinson expressed an interest in seeing Beman's plans, it is not known whether Beman submitted more detailed drawings to him, and there is no evidence that the Exposition's directors even considered Beman's plans or asked him to pursue them further.[9]

Root, on the other hand, was encouraged to pursue his project for the Art Institute. He began corresponding with Hutchinson about the proposed Art Institute building in August 1890.[10] The *Inland Architect and News Record* report of April 1889, that Burnham and Root were planning a $50,000 addition to their 1885–87 Art Institute building, suggests that the trustees were already considering an expansion to be designed by that firm before Chicago had been appointed the site of the Exposition.[11] If this was the case, then it was natural for the trustees to ask Burnham and Root to design the proposed larger structure. The mutually satisfying experience of planning two earlier buildings for the Art Institute had enabled Root and Hutchinson to develop a comfortable working relationship. As a member of the trustees' buildings and grounds committee of the University of Chicago, Hutchinson also worked closely with University architect Henry Ives Cobb (1859–1931) on plans for several buildings on the campus. Hutchinson had a great personal interest in architecture; in 1889, the American Institute of Architects made him an honorary member for his services furthering the architectural profession.[12]

On December 20, 1890, Root presented his project before the Art Institute trustees. His design was for a polychromed building in the Romanesque Revival style (fig. 2). The specifications included colored stone, mosaics, bas-reliefs, and brown terracotta roofing tiles. There were at least seven different drawings for the building, of varying degrees of completeness, including pencil sketches of elevations, floor plans, and finished

FIGURE 2. John Wellborn Root (1850–1891). First study for the Art Institute of Chicago, c. 1890 (unexecuted). Delineated by Paul Lautrup. Watercolor and pencil on paper, 55.5 × 115 cm. Gift of John Wellborn Root, Jr., 1945.

FIGURE 3. John Wellborn Root. "Facade of the Projected Art Museum," final design for the Art Institute, c. 1890 (unexecuted). Photo: H. Monroe, *John Wellborn Root: A Study of His Life and Work* (1896; Park Forest, IL, 1966), p. 254.

presentation drawings of various stages in the design (see fig. 3).[13] While Root's use of the Romanesque Revival had direct antecedents in his 1885–87 Art Institute building, his 1890 project revealed a greater degree of refinement—one paralleled in the late works of Henry Hobson Richardson (1838–1886) and foreshadowing the wave of classicism that, following the critical success of McKim, Mead and White's Boston Public Library designs (1887–95), would soon sweep public architecture. Root did not live to see his building constructed. He died suddenly of pneumonia on January 15, 1891, at the age of forty-one. In writing to Hutchinson on March 14, Root's widow, Dora, said that Root had considered the Art Institute project "the opportunity to give free expression to the poet—and artist within. . . . His whole soul was bent upon it."[14]

The dimensions of Root's design had been based on the budget that would have been augmented by an allocation from the Exposition directorate to the Palace of Fine Arts—a large, fireproof structure intended to house works of art worth millions of dollars from several countries. On February 20, 1891, however, the Exposition directors decided to move the Palace of Fine Arts to Jackson Park. Although Burnham originally intended to carry out his late partner's design for the Palace, he faltered in his resolve. On May 15, Burnham offered the project to Francis M. Whitehouse of Burling and Whitehouse.[15] But by the end of the month, Burnham had changed his mind again, giving the job to his new designer, Charles B. Atwood (1849–1895), who had arrived in April from New York.[16] By June, Atwood had completed the project. His design drew high praise.

The sculptor Augustus Saint-Gaudens exclaimed that Atwood's Palace of Fine Arts (fig. 4) was "the best thing done since the Parthenon."[17] Charles McKim, of the New York firm of McKim, Mead and White, telegraphed his congratulations to Burnham after seeing the design published in the September 5 issue of *Harper's Weekly*. Reassured by the critical success of Atwood's design, Burnham wrote to Charles Hutchinson on September 8, citing McKim's praise and suggesting that Atwood would be a good choice for the architect of the new Art Institute building.[18] Apparently, Burnham and his firm were no longer certain of the commission.

Meanwhile, the Art Institute trustees remained determined in their plans for a central location, even though this meant that they would have to accept a more modest contribution from the Exposition. Instead of the $500,000 that they would have received had they shared the Palace of Fine Arts in Jackson Park, the Art Institute would receive only $200,000 toward the construction of a building that would cost at least $600,000. The smaller building would temporarily house the meetings of the World's Congress Auxiliary that were to provide a more cerebral complement to the Fair. The Exposition directorate felt this building could be located on the lake front because a site away from the distractions of the Exposition would be more conducive to serious discourse and more convenient for travelers attending the various congresses.

In March 1891, Hutchinson and his friend Martin A. Ryerson, a wealthy Chicago attorney and Art Institute trustee, negotiated with the Common Council of Chicago for the right to use the site of the Illinois Inter-State Industrial Exposition building for their new museum. This building, designed by William Boyington (1818–1898) in 1873, had been intended as a temporary structure for the annual exhibitions of the state's industrial and agricultural products (fig. 5).[19] The Common Council ordinance of March 30, 1891, gave the city ownership of the proposed building, allowing the Art Institute occupancy for as long as it desired.[20] On June 4, with the site secured, the Art Institute trustees formed a building committee consisting of five members of the executive committee: president Hutchinson, Ryerson, Charles D. Hamill, John C. Black, and vice-president James H. Dole.

At a special meeting on June 10, the trustees discussed the proposed sale of their old building to the Chicago Club. John J. Glessner, Albert A. Sprague, and Adolphus C. Bartlett were appointed to a committee to discuss prices with the club. The fact that all three were Art Institute trustees and members of the Chicago Club typified the nexus between the elite group of Chicago businessmen who engaged in civic improvement projects.[21] The *Tribune*, in fact, commented on the proposed sale:

The Chicago Club has on its roster most of the prominent, public-spirited men of the city, a large number of whom also belong to the Art Institute, so that in reality some of them become both buyer and seller, and what is to the interest of the one is to the interest of the other.[22]

By December, the club agreed to pay the Art Institute $425,000 for the property.

FIGURE 4. Charles B. Atwood (1849–1895), for D. H. Burnham and Co. Palace of Fine Arts, World's Columbian Exposition, 1893, under construction. This building, which housed the collections of the Field Museum of Natural History from the close of the World's Fair until 1920, is now the Museum of Science and Industry.

FIGURE 5. William W. Boyington (1818–1898). Illinois Inter-State Industrial Exposition Building, 1873. This building was demolished to make way for the Art Institute building. Photo: J. W. Taylor, Chicago Historical Society.

The *Tribune* reported on June 17 that, in addition to the Palace of Fine Arts, "Mr. Atwood is also working out a design for [the Art Institute] building from sketches left by the late John W. Root." While it is probable that Atwood was working on a design for the Art Institute, there are no sources to substantiate that he was basing it on Root's earlier work. According to Burnham, Atwood was "personally responsible" for the design of over sixty buildings at the Exposition, and, as chief of construction, Burnham was also extremely busy.[23]

In addition, the national character of the Exposition had greatly altered the atmosphere in Chicago. In January 1891, the Exposition's board of architects, consist-ing of architects from the "Eastern establishment" and Chicago's most prominent architects, had agreed upon a "classical" style for the buildings around the Court of Honor in Jackson Park. Since Root and most of the Chicago architects still preferred the more colorful Romanesque Revival, the adoption of the "new" style can be attributed to the influence of the Eastern architects and to Burnham's enthusiastic reception of it after Root's death. French academic classicism, as taught at the Ecole des Beaux-Arts in Paris, had exerted a growing influence on American architects as it was incorporated into the curricula of American architectural schools. This influence was clearly evident in designs for the buildings around the Court of Honor, which, published in architectural and popular journals in advance of their construction, gradually affected public taste.

Sometime after the location of the Palace of Fine Arts had been changed to Jackson Park, the Art Institute trustees decided to consider firms other than Burnham's.

Since Root's death, Burnham's preoccupation with the Exposition may have motivated members of the Art Institute board to suggest other architects.

On August 28, the *Tribune* reported that Burnham's firm (D. H. Burnham and Company) and Shepley, Rutan and Coolidge of Boston had been invited to submit plans for an Art Institute building in a classical style. This development is puzzling. An invitational competition may have saved the trustees more time and money than an open one, but why they invited only two firms is unclear. Moreover, why did they invite firms relatively unpracticed in the academic classical style they had chosen? McKim, Mead and White, for example, was more accomplished in this style than either Burnham or Shepley, Rutan and Coolidge. By the date of the competition, McKim, Mead and White's Boston Public Library building was nearing completion, and their Agriculture Building on the Court of Honor at the Exposition was also classical. While Atwood had proven himself with the Palace of Fine Arts design, the competition's very existence suggests that the Art Institute trustees were not satisfied simply to give Burnham the commission.

Although they were based in Boston, Shepley, Rutan and Coolidge did not lack Chicago connections. Their firm had inherited much of the business of Henry Hobson Richardson, and they had completed many projects for Richardson, who was often bedridden during the last years of his life. During those years, George Foster Shepley (1860–1903) frequently traveled in Richardson's place, overseeing much of the firm's out-of-town business.[24] Between 1885 and 1887, he helped to complete three Chicago commissions: the John J. Glessner house, the Franklin MacVeagh house, and the Marshall Field Wholesale Store. These commissions were executed for prominent men who were in positions to recommend the firm to the Art Institute.

The social ties that Richardson had already established with the Glessners and with other Chicago families were further strengthened by marriages in his firm and in the firm of Shepley, Rutan and Coolidge. In 1886, shortly after Richardson's death, Shepley married Richardson's daughter; Charles Allerton Coolidge (1858–1936), in turn, married Shepley's sister. Coolidge's brother, Dr. Frederick S. Coolidge, married Eleanor Sprague, daughter of Albert A. Sprague, a member of the executive committee of the Art Institute board.[25]

Shepley, Rutan and Coolidge did not really need to rely upon these connections, however. Although they did not design any buildings for the Exposition, they often worked with Frederick Law Olmsted (1822–1903), the consulting landscape architect for the Fair. They were highly competent architects in their own right, and a large portion of their work had been institutional, including the Stanford University campus in Palo Alto, California (commissioned in 1888).

Directed by corporate businessmen regularly accustomed to making major business decisions, the invitational competition for the new Art Institute building proceeded quietly and without fanfare. On October 3, the members of the building committee, along with trustees Albert A. Sprague, Eliphalet W. Blatchford, George N. Culver, and David W. Irwin, met to go over the plans. After careful deliberation, the meeting was adjourned until two days later, when the architects were invited separately to explain their plans more thoroughly. The final decision of the building committee was announced at a special meeting of the trustees on October 17. The building committee report, dated October 8, was read, briefly summarizing the committee's activities during the past year. The committee expressed gratitude to all those architects who had submitted designs: Atwood and Shepley, Rutan and Coolidge, as well as Root, Beman, and Healy and Millet.[26] The brevity of the following statement from the October 17, 1891, committee meeting, announcing the selection of Shepley, Rutan and Coolidge, unfortunately typifies most of the written sources that might otherwise have enabled us to understand the requirements of the trustees and the means by which they were able to obtain their desired ends through the architects:

The architects chosen for this competition were Charles B. Atwood, the designer for the Columbian Exposition, and the firm of Shepley, Rutan and Coolidge, Boston. Both architects were put in possession of the ideas of the Committee, and the plans, with approximate estimates, have been submitted within the last week. The architects have been called before the Committee to explain the plans. Upon deliberate consideration your Committee unanimously recommends that the firm of Shepley, Rutan and Coolidge be employed as architects of the proposed building upon the Lake Front. October 8, 1891.[27]

Little remains of the drawings submitted for the competition. Atwood's sketches were returned to him, and he included them in the 1894 annual exhibition of the Chicago Architectural Sketch Club.[28] After Atwood's death, Burnham, apparently still in possession of the drawings, included them in the 1897 Chicago Architectural Club annual exhibition at the Art Institute.[29] No illustrations of these designs were ever published for the exhibitions, and no one knows what happened to them.

None of the competitive drawings by Shepley, Rutan and Coolidge survive, either, but a few reduced-scale photographs taken of the lost originals provide some clues (figs. 6, 10, 11).[30] In addition, the Art Institute has some early working drawings from January 1892, including one of the Michigan Avenue facade and a south elevation (figs. 14, 15).[31] Finally, two perspective engravings from January 1892 help to clarify the evolution of the design (see figs. 12, 13).[32] Reconstructing the development of the design through these images helps us to understand the trustees' manner of working with the architects on the early stages of the project.

The photographs of the competition drawings reveal that they were elaborate ink-and-wash renderings. They represent various aspects of a monumental domed building for which a complete set of drawings must have existed; all that remains are the north elevation (fig. 10), a longitudinal section (fig. 11), and a badly preserved plan (fig. 6).[33] These renderings are highly detailed and their carefully finished appearance can only be explained by their function as competition drawings. (The plan, for example, includes marble intarsia patterns for the floors.) Several elements, which appear in embryonic form in these drawings, were retained in the final design, and the subsequent engravings and working drawings illuminate the process of refinement they went through.

The fact that the only extant copies of the competition drawings remained in the archives of the architects and not those of the client indicates that they represent a very early stage of the design. As more refined versions were drawn, the "outdated" drawings would have been returned to the firm—probably to the Chicago office.[34] Although its spaces were to be slightly altered later, the competition plan (fig. 6) consists of an inner rectangle enclosing the auditorium and library and an outer rectangle which contains gallery spaces along the perimeter. Both rectangles are bisected along the east-west axis by a long corridor ending in an apsidal exhibition salon overlooking the lake and the Illinois Central Railroad tracks. *The Inland Architect and News Record* later described this salon as "somewhat like the *Hemeciécle* of the Academy of Fine Arts at Paris."[35] A domed staircase appears in the center of this central corridor and, to either side of it, temporary auditoria for the World's Congress Auxiliary were to be constructed. The vestiges of those auditoria appear on the plan in the semicircular "Lecture Hall" and "Library." The offices of the secretary and the

director were to occupy the square rooms flanking the central entrance, and a room for the trustees was projected adjacent to the apsidal exhibition salon.

A refined version of this plan, doubtlessly reflecting concerns voiced by the trustees, appeared in *The Inland Architect and News Record* in February 1892 (fig. 7). Narrow corridor galleries, replacing the four coat rooms, were inserted along the inner walls of the rectangular galleries to either side of the main axis. These corridors shared the exterior walls of the library and lecture hall. This change may have diminished the size of the original galleries somewhat, but it afforded more wall space for the display of objects. It is the type of practical refinement one might expect of a museum board, though one would think that the architects might have pointed out the potential inconvenience caused by the lack of coat rooms.[36] Yet another refinement appears in the reduced dimensions of the lecture hall and the library, which were contracted in order to provide storage and office space around their perimeters.

The grand scheme represented by this plan demonstrates that the trustees considered the building in long-range terms. In 1893, when the new building opened, its plan actually resembled the letter "E" (see fig. 8): the north and south wings were completed but most of the central part was still to be constructed, as were the lecture hall and library. This approach to building was in keeping with the trustees' development policy for the Art Institute and for other institutions whose building programs they supervised. In March 1891, Charles Hutchinson wrote to William Rainey Harper, president of the University of Chicago, about the campus building program: "It might be advisable to build some of the minor buildings first . . . until we [have] money in hand with which to build the more important buildings which are to stand as the expression of a great university."[37] In this spirit, the Art Institute trustees published the complete plans for the building in their 1894 annual report with the "projected" areas appearing in outline (fig. 9).

In addition to their role in determining the plan, the trustees seem to have found the question of the building's actual appearance a rich topic of discussion. After awarding the commission to Shepley, Rutan and Coolidge, the trustees debated alterations to the competition design, which was for a two-story, classical structure with a central dome, set upon a rusticated base. Their minutes note a meeting on January 7, 1892, of the committee on buildings and grounds at the newly opened Chicago offices of the architects.[38] The competi-

FIGURE 6. Shepley, Rutan and Coolidge. Plan of The Art Institute of Chicago, competition drawing, 1891. Photo: Shepley Bulfinch Richardson and Abbott, architects, Boston.

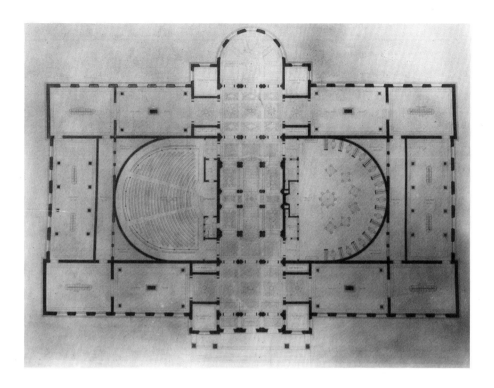

FIGURE 7. Shepley, Rutan and Coolidge. "Proposed Building for The Art Institute of Chicago," 1892. Photo: *Inland Architect and News Record* 19, 1 (Feb. 1892).

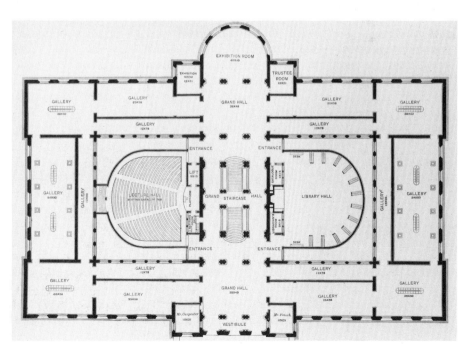

FIGURE 8. The Art Institute of Chicago under construction in 1892. Note the "E" shape
of the original building and the proximity of the Illinois Central Railroad tracks along the
lake shore. The tracks were spanned by Gunsaulus Hall in 1916. Photo: Chicago Historical
Society.

tion drawing of the north elevation (fig. 10), while more
ornate than the actual building, contains several elements that were retained in the final design. The overall
massing remained intact, but a number of decorative details were eliminated. In the base, the number of openings was reduced and they were simplified to rectangular
shapes punched out of the wall. The blind arcades of the
end pavilions were eventually reserved only for the
Michigan Avenue facade. The impost molding (at the
springing point of the arches) at the extreme right of the
right pavilion protrudes from the building in a manner
suggesting that the arcade continued around the corner
to the front of the building. This is confirmed by the
blind arcade on the facade of the later engraving. The
names of great artists which appear on the architrave (the
flat area of the entablature) above the second-story loggia would later run completely around the building.[39]

The longitudinal section that accompanied the north
elevation depicts the vaulted spaces of the central staircase, the library, and the lecture hall (fig. 11). Over the
central staircase, a hemispherical dome—surmounted by
a winged figure—rests on pendentives (the triangular

areas between the dome and its supporting piers). A
loggia runs around the upper story. Classical sculpture
appears in niches to either side of the staircase and a large
statue stands under the central arch of the loggia. Light
streams into the library and the lecture hall from the
windows piercing their vaults and the spaces behind the
curved ends of these areas conduct light and air into the
basement rooms below. For the Art Institute trustees,
the ornate grandeur of these proposed spaces must have
contrasted sharply with the familiar reality of their small
Romanesque Revival building three blocks south at Van
Buren Street.

Although the competition drawing for the Michigan
Avenue elevation is missing, an unpublished engraved
perspective (fig. 12, already mentioned) entitled "Proposed Building for The Art Institute of Chicago" from
January 1892 helps to suggest its probable appearance.
The silhouettes of the dome and the various rooflines in
the engraving match those of the competition drawing,
although the number and shape of the windows in the
first floor have been altered in the engraving. In addition, the arcades in the end pavilions of the north eleva-

FIGURE 9. Plan of the first floor of the Art Institute, as published in the *Annual Report* for 1894. The galleries in lighter line were proposed additions to the original structure; all were eventually completed except for the apsidal gallery proposed for the east side of the museum (shown at top of photo).

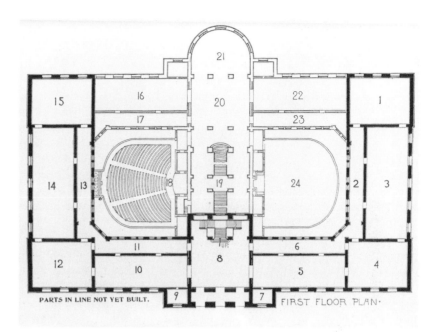

FIGURE 10. Shepley, Rutan and Coolidge. North elevation of The Art Institute of Chicago, competition drawing, 1891. Photo: Shepley Bulfinch Richardson and Abbott, architects, Boston.

tion were later discarded for sculptural friezes. On the second story of the entrance pavilion, on the north and south walls, the simple arched opening of the competition drawing has been replaced by a round window over a rectangular one. Such fussiness in the details of the later design suggests that the trustees were not entirely content with the continuous arcade of the competition design.

In this perspective, the entrance pavilion has an awkward, picturesque quality that interferes with the overall classical proportions of the facade and that recalls Root's earlier project. Most likely, the trustees found this entrance troublesome since it is absent from the second engraving of the facade (fig. 13) and from the finished building (see note 32). On the other hand, in terms of the initial competition design, such superficial resemblances to Root's project may have operated in favor of the Boston firm.

A published copy of the second version bears the same caption as the first version (fig. 12). The only explanation for these two different versions bearing the same title is that they were printed before the trustees had reached a final decision on the design. For this reason, the engravings must date to shortly before the January 7, 1892, meeting. The primary difference between the two en-

gravings lies in the entrance pavilions and the rooflines: the dome and the gabled entrance of the one contrasts sharply with the saddleback roofs and the entrance pediment of the other. With these exceptions, the wings flanking the center of either engraving are identical, with seven bays on each side. Even minute background details are the same, suggesting that the central portion of the plate was reworked, or otherwise replaced, from one print to another. While there can be little question that the design in the domed perspective is the older of the two, the sculpted friezes appearing on the end pavilions in both engravings are new features added in place of the arcades that wrapped around the building in the competition designs.

The sculpted friezes figure prominently in two working drawings, one of the western elevation and one of the southern elevation (figs. 14, 15). They depict a much simpler building with a central pediment, and the drawings are austere compared to the competition drawings. The panels that replace the blind arcade of the original scheme, and that were included in the final building, were intended for sculpture: those friezes that were executed reproduce parts of the Panathenaic procession from the Parthenon.[40]

The panels in the working drawings represent an intermediate stage between the competition drawings and the engravings. Therefore, it is possible that the working drawings were prepared as early as late December 1891 and possibly before the engravings of early January. Shepley, Rutan and Coolidge did not occupy either office given in the addresses on the drawings before that

FIGURE 11. Shepley, Rutan and Coolidge. Longitudinal section of The Art Institute of Chicago, competition drawing, 1891. Photo: Shepley Bulfinch Richardson and Abbott, architects, Boston.

time.[41] Meeting again on January 8 in the architects' office, the building committee discussed the best manner for letting contracts. One of the working drawings refers to a contract concerning the building, perhaps a topic of conversation at the January 7 meeting: "This part of the roof not included in this contract/ also chimney" appears on the southern elevation drawing (fig. 15). The vote of the governing members on January 22 to approve the erection of the new building would seem to indicate that all formal arrangements with the architects were in order, further confirming the early January dates for both the engravings and working drawings. On February 5, the committee on buildings and grounds elected to contract with Jonathan Clark and Company for demolition of the Inter-State Industrial Exposition building and for the construction of the new Art Institute.

FIGURE 12. Shepley, Rutan and Coolidge. "Proposed Building for The Art Institute of Chicago," 1892. This photograph of a now-lost engraved perspective view shows an early design for the museum. Photo: Shepley Bulfinch Richardson and Abbott, architects, Boston.

FIGURE 13. Shepley, Rutan and Coolidge. "The Art Institute of Chicago," 1892. This photograph of a now-lost engraved perspective view shows the museum as it was built. Photo: Shepley Bulfinch Richardson and Abbott, architects, Boston.

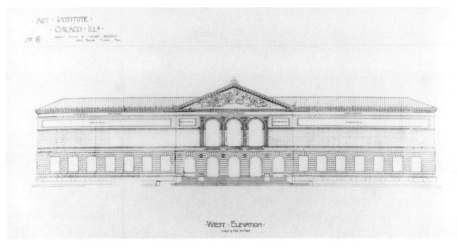

FIGURE 14. Shepley, Rutan and Coolidge. West elevation of the Art Institute, working drawing, 1892. Ink on linen.

FIGURE 15. Shepley, Rutan and Coolidge. South elevation of the Art Institute, working drawing, 1892. Ink on linen.

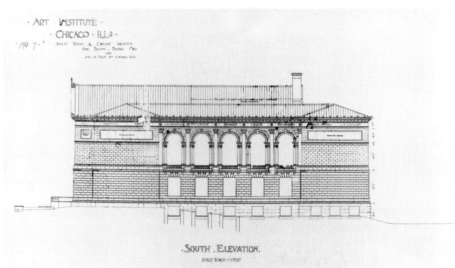

In late September 1891, as Shepley, Rutan and Coolidge were preparing competitive designs for the Art Institute, the directors of the Chicago Public Library invited them to submit a project to the competition for their proposed building, on Michigan Avenue several blocks north of the site of the new Art Institute. The Library designs were due before noon on January 2, 1892.[42] So, both Art Institute and Public Library designs were "on the boards" at the same time in the Boston office of the firm. The winning design (fig. 16) for the Library, by Shepley, Rutan and Coolidge, shares two notable characteristics with the Art Institute's. First, the glazed arcade on the first floor of the Library bears a striking resemblance to the blind arcade on the facade of the Art Institute. This type of arcade was not unique to these two projects, however, for it had precedent in much earlier buildings,[43] and McKim, Mead and White

had used it in their designs for the Boston Public Library. Second, both arcades have symbolic roundels in the spandrels above the arches. Moreover, both buildings have names inscribed on their architraves (see figs. 16, 17). There is no evidence to suggest collaboration between the trustees of the two institutions since the membership of the two boards did not coincide. The directors of the Library were drawn from the community at large and not from the elite group comprising the Art Institute trustees. In that the Public Library did not award the commission to Shepley, Rutan and Coolidge until February 11, the Art Institute designs clearly came first.

These details help to indicate the architects' role in formulating the iconography of what were, for both institutions, buildings of unprecedented scale and type in Chicago. The facades of both buildings clearly indicate their purpose. Through inscriptions and sculpture, they provide the history of literature and of the fine arts the public would encounter inside. In discussing the proposed competition for their new building, the Public Library directors stated explicitly that "the exterior shall to a degree make known the purpose of the building."[44] It is hard to believe that the Art Institute trustees would not have been equally explicit, even if no written record exists to verify it. The chronologically arranged names of painters, sculptors, and architects running around the Art Institute entablature found their counterpart in the names of great authors grouped chronologically and according to national origin on the Public Library.[45] These characteristics, in turn, reflected the directors' and trustees' conceptions of collection display and order. The theories underlying the arrangement of books or art objects had become disciplines in their own right during the nineteenth century. The new "Temple of Culture" rising on the banks of Lake Michigan was a monument to the values and preconceptions of the men who oversaw its execution. By the same token, the architects saw the academic classical style as a suitable expression for an enduring institution such as the Art Institute, as well as symbolic of the ancient authority of western classical culture.

Shepley, Rutan and Coolidge themselves occasionally suggested minor changes while erecting the Public Library building. In this manner, they often improved the efficiency of the design and saved their clients money.[46] There can be no question that the Art Institute trustees were treated with the same consideration. Few records remain of the earliest transactions between the Art Institute trustees and Shepley, Rutan and Coolidge, but subsequent commissions for the Art Institute and for the

FIGURE 17. View of a portion of the south facade of the Art Institute showing names of artists inscribed on the architrave.

University of Chicago under the supervision of Hutchinson and Ryerson provide a clear idea of a mutually sympathetic and profitable working relationship.[47]

The best testimony of the trustees' continued satisfaction with Shepley, Rutan and Coolidge lies in the ten projects executed for the Art Institute by the firm and its successors. As early as 1894, the year following the Art Institute's occupation of the new building, Shepley, Rutan and Coolidge were working on completing the long-range plans. Two drawings of a domed termination to the Grand Staircase embody the trustees' conception of the new grandeur appropriate to the future they intended for their institution.[48] Shepley, Rutan and Coolidge helped them to visualize that grandeur. In "Proposed Additions to The Art Institute of Chicago," a dome of more elegant proportions than the one in the competition drawings rises over the pedimented entrance. An oculus replaces the sculpture on top, and the stepped drum creates a more gradual transition from the pediment than the awkward cylinder of the dome in the competition drawing.[49] In the 1894 project, the remains of some effaced pencil strokes above the dome suggest a discussion between the architects and clients about raising its profile.

A section of the interior delineated by Robert C. Spencer, Jr., by far the most beautiful and ornate of any

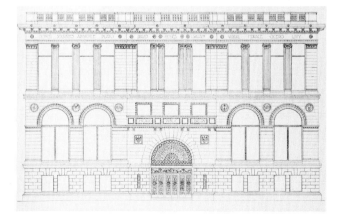

FIGURE 16. Shepley, Rutan and Coolidge. "Accepted Competition Design for the Chicago Public Library," 1892, elevation. Photo: *Inland Architect and News Record* 19, 2 (Mar. 1892).

of the drawings, survives in a photograph (fig. 18).[50] Light streams in through an oculus in the saucer dome. The height of the overall composition has been lowered to correspond with the shallower dome. Some of the details reflect this change. In the competition section, an arch spanned the piers supporting the upper floor. This arch, along with the pilasters that decorated the piers, was abandoned in the 1894 section. The entire composition is simpler and more compact.

The larger scale of the 1894 section renders the decoration more legible. The intrados (underside of the dome) and pendentives are covered with frescoes. The intrados has painted coffers, with panels including the names of artists. The spandrels above the loggia bear allegorical frescoes similar to those in the competition section. Moreover, casts of classical sculpture appear in both. Several of those depicted in Spencer's drawing are identifiable as casts from the Art Institute's Elbridge G. Hall Collection.[51] This careful arrangement of the sculpture casts in the drawing suggests that the trustees had considered the iconography of the composition very carefully, to the extent that specific elements of the design had possibly been dictated to the architects. The cast of the Nike of Samothrace perched in the center of the staircase loggia has clear associations with the location of the original in the Daru Staircase of the Musée du Louvre in Paris. Hutchinson and French would have seen the statue in this context on their 1889 tour of European museums.[52] Spencer's rendering represents a more carefully considered decorative program than the generic winged figure in the corresponding area of the competition section. Similarly, the elevation and carefully detailed section of the 1894 design represent a more mature classicism than that of its 1891 ancestor.

In this sense, the development of the Art Institute design expresses the increasing familiarity of the trustees and of Shepley, Rutan and Coolidge with the new architectural language that they had chosen to represent their institution. The comfortable working relationship that the trustees had enjoyed earlier with John Root was transferred to Charles A. Coolidge. Coolidge moved to Prairie Avenue in 1892, becoming a neighbor to as well as an architect for several trustees. Just as they had customarily turned to Root for professional assistance, after the 1891 commission, they relied on Coolidge. Even after Coolidge returned to Boston in 1900, Hutchinson and Ryerson continued to call upon him for assistance with the building programs of the Art Institute and the University of Chicago.[53]

Years of working together on extensive building programs for two of Chicago's most important cultural institutions created strong bonds of trust and friendship between Coolidge, Hutchinson, and Ryerson. When the University administration became dissatisfied with Henry Ives Cobb, Shepley, Rutan and Coolidge replaced him as University architects. Working closely with Ryerson, Hutchinson, and the trustees' committee on buildings and grounds, Shepley, Rutan and Coolidge designed nearly every building on the campus for twenty years.[54] The firm's extensive service to the University confirms their satisfactory relationship with the trustees. After the deaths of George Shepley (1903) and Charles Rutan (1914), Coolidge continued to work through the Chicago office, in partnership with Charles Hodgdon (originally from the Boston office), for the University and the Art Institute. A 1923 letter from Hodgdon to University president Edwin DeWitt Burton in response to an inquiry about a contract suggests the trust underlying many years of satisfactory work based on mutual understanding between architects and clients:

This agreement, as well as every agreement we have had with the University that I can now recall, is oral, Mr. Ryerson and Mr. Hutchinson . . . having said that our terms were accepted, and ever since we have proceeded on those terms.[55]

Hodgdon's comments perhaps explains the lack of documents about the early Art Institute projects.

Lacking those documents, the drawings of the early stages of the design must speak for the trustees and the architects who together saw the Allerton Building as an unparalleled opportunity. Nothing comparable to the Allerton Building had been erected before in Chicago. The new building depicted in the early drawings projected a more sophisticated image for the Art Institute, raising the perceived level of culture of "newly arrived" Chicago. The academic classical language of the building reflected that new urbanity. Small details, such as the names of great artists on the entablature, suggested a more systematic approach to the display of the museum's growing collections. The very style of the building, which the trustees knew as Italian Renaissance, was the architectural language used to express the functions of many major European museums.

The new building program, looking to the future and incorporating inevitable growth, was inaugurated by the Allerton Building. In choosing Shepley, Rutan and

FIGURE 18. Shepley, Rutan and Coolidge. Interior perspective view of proposed staircase and dome for the Art Institute, 1894 (unexecuted). This ink and wash drawing, delineated by Robert C. Spencer, Jr., is now lost.

Coolidge, the Art Institute trustees found a firm sympathetic to their needs and able to satisfy them. And in Charles A. Coolidge, who served as the firm's primary liaison with the board, both Charles Hutchinson and Martin Ryerson discovered an associate with whom they would develop long-lasting friendships.

At a time when American architects were coming to regard themselves as well-trained professionals charged with the task of elevating public taste, a commission like the Art Institute served as an excellent opportunity to demonstrate the superiority of their formal training. The architecture of cultural and educational institutions could influence society in ways analogous to those of the institutions themselves. The Art Institute commission enabled Shepley, Rutan and Coolidge to work in a style deemed appropriate for monumental public buildings.

At the same time, it served as an introduction to a group of men whose activities as architectural patrons have rarely been equaled in any other American city.

In choosing to erect their building in an academic classical style, the Art Institute trustees exerted a definitive influence over future buildings for cultural institutions in Chicago.[56] While the buildings of the World's Columbian Exposition were ephemeral, the Art Institute building was not. The trustees' insistence on locating their new building adjacent to the city's commercial center indicates that they were concerned with larger issues of urban development. Facing the soot-blackened office buildings lining Michigan Avenue, the new Art Institute represented the best hopes and efforts of Chicago businessmen to transform the face of their city into something fine and beautiful.

The Art Institute's Guardian Lions

JANE H. CLARKE, *Associate Director of Museum Education*

Among the most famous works of art in the Art Institute's collections is the pair of bronze lions (fig. 1) standing guard at the main entrance to the museum on Michigan Avenue. Unveiled on May 10, 1894, the pair was adopted almost instantaneously by Chicagoans as a proud symbol of the city's prestigious art museum. Over the years, the lions, by American sculptor Edward L. Kemeys (1843–1907), have come to symbolize the city of Chicago itself, appearing as landmarks on tourist maps and guidebook covers. In innumerable newspaper cartoons, they have been made to comment on city affairs. The Christmas season in Chicago seems to begin when they don their wreaths, and enthusiastic sports fans have turned them into mascots for winning Chicago teams by crowning them with Bears helmets and Cubs caps (see fig. 2). Despite our familiarity with these two sculptures, most of us know little about their creator and the circumstances of their commission.[1]

Lions as guardians have an ancient history. The fierceness, strength, and grace of the regal animal led the earliest human rulers to adopt it as a symbol of royalty and of guardianship. The Lion Gate at Mycenae (c. 1300 B.C.), the parade of striding lions on the walls of Babylon (sixth century B.C.), and Emperor Asoka's lion columns in India (c. 240 B.C.) are only a few examples. Throughout the Near and Far East, the lion image was incorporated into works of jade and other stones, bronze, and precious metals, as well as into mosaics and painted miniatures. The Crusaders in the Middle Ages returned from the Middle East with the lion as a heraldic device. The animal's popularity as a visual image recurred during the Italian Renaissance,

FIGURE 1. The Michigan Avenue entrance of The Art Institute of Chicago with its two guardian lions by Edward Kemeys (1843–1907).

47

FIGURE 2. In 1986, the Art Institute's famous lions, in addition to their customary holiday season wreaths, sported Chicago Bears football helmets in anticipation of the team's appearance in Super Bowl XX.

and was again revived in the nineteenth century by such Romantic artists as Antoine Louis Barye (1796–1875), the noted French *animalier* (animal sculptor).

The Art Institute lions, along with the pair in front of the New York Public Library and in the grand staircase of the Boston Public Library, are a late example of this tradition. Fascinated with animal life, many nineteenth-century artists followed the explorations of naturalists in distant or remote parts of the world or avidly frequented zoological parks. The French painter Rosa Bonheur actually kept a caged lion in her studio. Wildlife appealed to the Romantic imagination not only because it seemed exotic, but also because it expressed to them the raw passions and drives that civilization had repressed in man. Kemeys admired Barye and undoubtedly attended the 1889 exhibition of his work in New York. The Art Institute's African lions show the influence of the formally trained French artist on the self-taught American.

The general perception has long been that the Art Institute lions were derived from two lions by Kemeys which stood at the north entrance of the Palace of Fine Arts at the World's Columbian Exposition (see figs. 3, 4). But their lineage is not entirely clear, and plans for the art palace and the 1893 Art Institute building are inextricably bound together (see Phipps, pp. 28–45). The Art Institute was founded in 1879 as The Chicago Academy of Fine Arts, officially adopted the name of The Art Institute of Chicago in 1882, and moved into a new building designed by Burnham and Root at the corner of Michigan and Van Buren in 1887 (see Chronology, p. 8, fig. 4). The 1891 *Annual Report* of the Art Institute trustees summarizes the expanding programs of the School and museum and indicates that its four-year-old build-

FIGURE 3. View of the World's Columbian Exposition, showing a portion of the Court of Honor and the Agricultural Building (McKim, Mead and White, architects), 1893. The panther at the lower right was sculpted by Kemeys.

ing was no longer large enough for their activities.[2] The advent of the World's Columbian Exposition presented a golden opportunity to gain larger quarters. The trustees supported a plan to erect for the Exposition one permanent building to serve as the fair's art palace, which would later become the new Art Institute, and stand as a memorial to the Exposition.

Thus, from the beginning, the Art Institute was involved with the planning for the Exposition's Palace of Fine Arts. And, since Charles L. Hutchinson, president of the museum's Board of Trustees from 1882 until his death in 1924, was also chairman of the Department of Fine Arts of the Exposition, it was to remain involved. When the Board of Directors of the Exposition finally decided in February of 1891 upon an Exposition site in Jackson Park, seven miles to the south of the downtown area, the Art Institute trustees debated whether to build the new Art Institute building on the fair site or on Michigan Avenue in Lake Park. The trustees wanted to build on Michigan Avenue, near the center of the city, and still have the support of the Exposition, but the Exposition directors were opposed to placing the art palace several miles from the fair. A cooperative plan among the City of Chicago's civic bodies made possible the final agreement for a permanent building to be constructed on the Lake Park site to house the World's Congresses during the fair, after which the building would revert to the Art Institute.[3] A separate Palace of Fine Arts would be raised on the Exposition site. This decision early in 1891 effectively made Charles L. Hutchinson the client for two art museums being built simultaneously, probably a unique episode in the history of museum architecture in America.

Guardian lions were ordained for both art museums early in the design stages. In September 1891, a drawing of the proposed art palace for the Exposition appeared in *Harper's Weekly*, including a pair of lions at the entrance.[4] The architect of this design was Charles B. Atwood, a Beaux-Arts trained architect from New York who came to Chicago in April 1891 at the invitation of Daniel H. Burnham, the Exposition's Chief of Construction. Atwood was named Designer in Chief for the Exposition, and discussions concerning the art palace must have begun immediately with Burnham, Atwood, and Hutchinson because, according to art historian Ann Van Zanten, Atwood designed the fine-arts building in "about a month" after coming to Chicago.[5] This dates Atwood's drawing of the fine-arts palace to sometime in May or June of 1891. The February 1892 issue of *The Inland Architect and News Record* included an engraved perspective view labeled "Proposed Building for The Art Institute of Chicago," by the Boston architectural firm Shepley, Rutan and Coolidge, complete with lions at the entrance. This same engraving appeared at the frontispiece to the *Annual Report of the Trustees for the Year Ending June 7, 1892*, with the caption "The Art Institute. Now in process of erection on the Lake Front" (fig. 5). Hutchinson obviously had been closely involved in all the design decisions for both Atwood's Exposition building and the Art Institute.

Hutchinson was also closely involved with Atwood in the elaborate sculptural program for the Palace of Fine Arts. They soon had many artists to choose from. Among the sculptors attracted to Chicago by the opportunity

FIGURE 4. One of a pair of lions by Kemeys at the north entrance of the Palace of Fine Arts (Charles B. Atwood for D.H. Burnham and Co., architects), the World's Columbian Exposition, 1893. These lions were probably the models for the Art Institute's lions.

FIGURE 5. Shepley, Rutan and Coolidge, architects. Perspective view of The Art Institute of Chicago, published as the frontispiece to the museum's 1892 *Annual Report* with the caption "Now in process of erection on the Lake Front."

to create works that would be seen by thousands of visitors to the fair were Augustus Bauer, Karl Bitter, Daniel Chester French, Johannes Gelert, Edward Kemeys, Frederick William MacMonnies, Philip Martiny, Hermon A. McNeil, Edward Clark Potter, A. Phimister Proctor, Louis St. Gaudens, M.A. Wagoner, and Olin L. Warner. Any of these sculptors might have been candidates for Hutchinson's choice for the Art Institute lions. Martiny, in fact, was assigned much exterior decoration of the fine-arts palace, including copies of parts of the Parthenon frieze, which he also made for the north and south facades of the Art Institute.

Exactly how the various sculptors were assigned projects at the Exposition can only be guessed at. Included in Burnham's 1893 *Report of the Director of*

FIGURE 6. View of the World's Columbian Exposition Court of Honor, 1893, showing the many animal figures that were part of the sculptural program at the fair.

Works is a report by F. D. Millet, who had been on the Exposition staff from the beginning and who became, on June 1, 1892, director of the fair's Department of Decoration. Millet stated that the decorative scheme was "necessarily, somewhat vague. . . . The possible field for decorative sculpture was, at the date above mentioned, only partially filled."[6] He went on to say that contracts had already been let to two sculptors, Edward Kemeys and A.P. Proctor, "for models of native animals of North America, to be set upon pedestals of the bridges [see fig. 6]. A studio was furnished each of these parties in the Horticultural Building" (see figs. 9, 10).[7]

Millet did not supervise the decoration without advice and consent from others. He was a member of the artistic council which Burnham constantly consulted, "to which were referred all important artistic questions, and in whose hands was the account of the various designs." In 1891, the committee consisted of Atwood, Millet, and Henry Sargent Codman.[8] Codman, chief landscape architect for the fair, died suddenly in January 1892, which left only Millet and Atwood, with the latter a key figure. There was a third adviser, although not on the committee: Charles McKim of the distinguished New York architectural firm of McKim, Mead, and White, and designer of a number of fair buildings. "He was in many ways the artistic conscience for Daniel Burnham, the grand master of the undertaking, advising him on color, sculpture and architecture."[9] It can be assumed that Hutchinson, Atwood, Burnham, Millet, and probably McKim, met frequently to discuss the sculptural program in general, and, in particular, for the Palace of Fine Arts, one of the most important buildings at the fair. The program included a number of pairs of lions by several of the sculptors listed above.

Lions by E. C. Potter (fig. 7) graced the entrance of McKim's New York State building on the "beautiful and commanding site opposite the Art Palace."[10] McKim was probably directly involved with the ornamentation, having selected the "Italian Renaissance" style for the building, modeled on the Villa Medici in Rome. Potter's lions, too, have a specific source: in the relief sculptures built into the walls of the staircase landing of the Palazzo Barberini in Rome. A cast of the original relief was made in 1891 and reached the United States "shortly before the New York State Building was designed." Potter was given the difficult task of turning the relief into the round for his models, which he was thought to have accomplished with great success.[11]

Potter was Beaux-Arts trained and worked extensively on other sculptures at the fair with Daniel Chester French, brother of Art Institute director William M. R. French. Potter's close working relationship with French, in addition to his equally close association with McKim, would surely have been a recommendation to Hutchinson for the Art Institute lions. The Renaissance source of Potter's lions was also in keeping with the generally Renaissance style of Shepley, Rutan and Coolidge's design for the Art Institute on Michigan Avenue.

Directly facing the State of New York building stood the Palace of Fine Arts. Six pairs of lions guarded the entrances: one pair each at the principal, south entrance and at the secondary, north entrance, as well as a pair at the east and west entrances of the building's two annexes. The lions at the south

FIGURE 7. View of the south entrance of the New York State Building (McKim, Mead and White, architects), the World's Columbian Exposition, 1893. The pair of lions by Edward Potter (1857–1923) faced those at the north entrance of the Palace of Fine Arts.

FIGURE 8. View of the south entrance of the Palace of Fine Arts, the World's Columbian Exposition, showing lions by A. Phimister Proctor (1862–1950).

FIGURE 9. Kemeys and his wife, Laura Swing Kemeys, in their temporary studio in the Horticultural Building, the World's Columbian Exposition, c. 1893. Mrs. Kemeys was an accomplished sculptor in her own right and worked closely with her husband. The panther they are working on can be seen in place in fig. 10.

entrance (fig. 8) were sculpted by A. Phimister Proctor. Proctor, at thirty-seven, was relatively young and unknown before the fair, so he was probably not seriously considered by Hutchinson for the Art Institute commission. Very little is known about Augustus Bauer, sculptor of the annex lions. His couchant lions were described in Burnham's final report as "a little conventionalized, perhaps, but without sacrificing the force and majesty of this royal beast."[12] Earning such faint praise, Bauer was also probably not considered by Hutchinson.

The sixth pair of lions, standing at the north entrance to the Palace of Fine Arts (see fig. 4), were by Edward Kemeys. Kemeys was a self-proclaimed, self-taught American sculptor whose oeuvre was dedicated to memorializing the already vanishing wildlife of his native land.[13] In his *History of American Sculpture*, first published in 1903, the noted Chicago sculptor Lorado Taft wrote that Kemeys's works were part of "the slow unfolding of a national art . . . he recognizes the artistic possibilities of our own land and time."[14] Kemeys became a sculptor at the age of twenty-six with no previous training, and recognition followed with astonishing speed. In interviews in *Century* and *McClure's* magazines and in various newspapers, Kemeys told of an almost mystical experience that directed him to his artistic career.[15] After serving in the Union Army during the Civil War, he was employed for two dollars a day as an axeman on the engineering corps working on the wilderness terrain that was being turned into Frederick Law Olmsted and Calvert Vaux's masterpiece, Central Park (1856–76). In his reminiscences, Kemeys said that he took pleasure in observing the wild animals in the area and in the small Central Park zoo, where one day in 1869 he observed an old German sculptor modeling the head of a wolf. "Quick as lightning came the thought . . . 'I can do that!' "[16] As soon as Kemeys could get hold of some modeling material, he began working on a head of a wolf himself and his future was determined. Only three years after his experience in Central Park, Kemeys's proposal for a sculpture for Fairmount Park in Philadelphia was accepted.[17] *Two Hudson Bay Wolves Quarreling Over the Carcass of a Deer* still stands in the Philadelphia Zoological Gardens adjacent to Wolf Woods.

This first success enabled Kemeys to fulfill a dream: to make an extended trip to the West in 1872–73.[18] There he began his study of wild animals in their native habitat. He hunted, dissected the game he shot to analyze its skeletal and muscle structure, lived with Indians, made friends with old trappers, and began his lifelong work of recording this mythic aspect of the American experience.

It was small, cast bronzes of his animal subjects (see fig. 11) that brought Kemeys to the attention of Chicagoans. In May 1885, the Art Institute held a special exhibition of American "Wild Animals and Indians" by Kemeys. The exhibition included forty-six models in plaster, clay, and bronze, along with engravings and "twenty three sheets of rough sketches, notes and studies made by Mr. Kemeys in mountain and plain, and an original drawing by a Crow Indian."[19] The catalogue notes that a price list was available in the office; presumably, some of the works were sold out of the exhibition. Sales of Kemeys's works made possible more trips to the West, which in turn made possible more sculptures. "I'd go back to New York and work till I sold something, and then—back West again."[20] With a well-publicized career and works in the Art Institute collections[21] and private Chicago collections, Kemeys was a natural to be invited to work on the fair and to be considered by Hutchinson for the Art Institute lions.

One of Kemeys's Chicago patrons was Bryan Lathrop, a trustee of the Art Institute. It is probably his recommendation of Kemeys to Hutchinson, along with Kemeys's familiarity to Chicagoans, that gave him the advantage in obtaining the Art Institute commission. The following letter from Lathrop to Hutchinson, dated September 24, 1892, makes it clear that the artist was highly recommended and states a proposal for the acquisition of the lions for the Art Institute entrance.[22]

My dear Mr. Hutchinson

I sent you a dispatch on Thursday evening, asking you to make no contract for the bronze lions for the Art Institute building until you got a letter from me.

I have been delighted with Kemeys's work, both at the World's Fair and with that which he has done with me. I had some talk with him about the lions which you have proposed to have in bronze, at the entrance of the building, as I understand, and I got the impression that you hesitated about awarding the work to him, as there was someone else whom you had considered with reference to it.

I have a very strong conviction that there is no other animal sculptor in this country at all to be compared with Kemeys, and if there is any who is his equal now living anywhere I do not know about him. I am therefore very anxious to have him execute the bronze lions.

I am greatly interested in the Art Institute as the chief exponent of art in Chicago, and I think that the two bronzes in front of the building will do much to educate the popular taste for what is good art, provided that they are really admirable works of art.

With all that in mind I talked with my sister, Mrs. Henry Field, about the matter. She has entered into the subject very heartily, and she is equally anxious to have Kemeys intrusted with the commission. Mr. Field admired Kemeys's work very much and liked Mr. Kemeys personally.

FIGURE 10. View of Kemeys's studio and two of his figures for the World's Fair. Kemeys first made small-scale models of his figures before enlarging them to life size. Photo: Michael Richman.

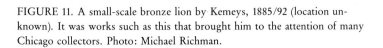

FIGURE 11. A small-scale bronze lion by Kemeys, 1885/92 (location unknown). It was works such as this that brought him to the attention of many Chicago collectors. Photo: Michael Richman.

Mrs. Field knows that her husband had the interests of the Art Institute very much at heart, and that he would have very much liked to have the bronze lions made by Kemeys: and she therefore decided, if agreeable to yourself and the Art Institute, to present them to the Art Institute, on condition that she can have them designed by Mr. Kemeys and cast under his directions, and that she be allowed to pass upon the designs. The Art Institute could of course reserve the right to accept or reject them even after they have been executed.

I should be obliged if you would telegraph me on receipt of this whether you have made any contract for the lions or not, so that I can at once communicate with Kemeys. Mrs. Field would prefer not to have her name mentioned at present or made public in any way. Her main idea is to give these lions as a sort of memento of her husband.

I write in haste for this mail.

Sincerely yours,
Bryan Lathrop

There is no record of Hutchinson's reply to this missive, nor is it possible to know who else he had in mind for the commission, but events apparently moved swiftly, for on January 31, 1893, the minutes of the Executive Committee of the Art Institute's Board of Trustees record that "the president then stated that Mrs. Henry Field had presented to The Art Institute of Chicago two bronze lions to be executed by Mr. Kemeys."[23] The committee voted to accept the gift and to thank the donor. The fourteenth annual report of the trustees, issued in June 1893, announced that Mrs. Henry Field "had previously authorized the trustees to order at her expense from Mr. Edward Kemeys, the animal sculptor, two monumental bronze lions to stand upon the flanks of the great external entrance stairway of the new museum. The order has been given to Mr. Kemeys and he is at work upon the models, for which the pedestals stand ready."[24]

It is clear that Kemeys's commission for the Art Institute's bronze lions was the result of his familiarity to Lathrop and to Mr. and Mrs. Field. Less certain is the relative timing of the decisions made by Hutchinson and the others involved for both the Art Institute and the Palace of Fine Arts commissions. After listing Kemeys's and Proctor's bridge sculptures as already decided upon in August 1892, Millet had also commented that "later in the season," Proctor executed "lions for the main pedestals of the Art Building."[25] He did not mention Kemeys's pair at the secondary north entrance.[26] When Hutchinson accepted Kemeys as the sculptor of Mrs. Field's proposed gift to the Art Institute sometime soon after Lathrop's letter of September 21, 1892, it is entirely possible that he suggested that Kemeys create the additional pair for the art palace. If this is true, then Mrs. Field's commission for the Art Institute led to the Palace of Fine Arts lions by Kemeys, and that the fair lions, which of necessity had to be finished before the opening on

May 1, 1893, became the models for the Art Institute bronzes. In fact, the large staff (a combination of plaster of paris, hemp fibers, and portland cement) pieces made by Kemeys for the Exposition were used to make the molds for casting the Art Institute's bronzes.[27] It is also uncertain whether Proctor's design for the pair at the south entrance of the art palace influenced Kemeys's lions or vice versa, as the pairs are strikingly similar.

The Exposition closed on October 31, 1893. On December 8, Art Institute members attended a gala opening of their new museum with memories of the fair fresh in their minds, and the lions were officially unveiled on May 10, 1894. The reception of the lions was enthusiastic; they are considered today among Kemeys's finest achievements. Like his many pairs of native American animals, these African lions are not identical. Their heads, tails, and stances are different: In Kemeys's words, the lion to the north of the Art Institute steps is "on the prowl" (see fig. 12), while the lion to the south stands "in an attitude of defiance" (see fig. 13). The sculptor described his defiant lion as one of "the most difficult I have ever attempted."[28] Kemeys and his wife were honored at a reception the evening of May 10, in conjunction with the opening of the annual Chicago Architectural Sketch Club exhibition. Among the sketches exhibited were drawings by Charles Atwood for his proposals for the Art Instititue (see Phipps, pp. 28–45), and nearby were small sculptures by Kemeys that were part of the Art Institute's collections.

Kemeys remained in Chicago after the Exposition closed and established a residence that included a large studio building. For the first few years the outlook for the sculptor seemed promising. Small bronzes of his sculptures were in demand, and, in 1894, the Winslow Bros. Company, a Chicago foundry, published a brochure advertising their availability upon order.[29] Kemeys's activities in Chicago went beyond his sculptural commissions. He was a popular lecturer, and his colorful interviews certainly indicate that his audiences were well entertained. A brochure for his lectures called *Art and Inspiration of Mountain and Plains . . . Edward Kemeys Sculptor*, appeared in 1896–97.[30] By the end of the 1890s, Kemeys's commissions were dwindling and he and his wife returned to the East around 1900, settling in Washington, D.C. Kemeys died there in 1907.

With the installation of the lions, a permanent link between the Art Institute and the temporary Palace of Fine Arts was realized. By that time, there was a treasure inside the Art Institute worthy of their guardianship, also the gift of Mrs. Field. The museum had received the most important accession in its fourteen-year history: the entire collection of paintings which belonged to the late Henry Field. Although the original intention of making the Art Institute building a memorial to the Exposition was never carried out, the museum's lions are in a sense that memorial: The guardians of the temporary art palace still stand as permanent guardians at the principal entrance of the Art Institute.

FIGURES 12, 13. Close-up views of the Art Institute's lions. Above is the lion to the north of the museum entrance; below is the lion to the south.

FIGURE 1. Aerial view from the southeast of The Art Institute of Chicago complex, 1984. Photo: Tigerhill Studio.

The Art Institute Expands: Challenges of Mid-Century

ROBERT BRUEGMANN, *University of Illinois at Chicago*

I. The Competition of 1934

Like many American art museums founded in the nineteenth century, the physical plant of the Art Institute started to grow at an ever-accelerating rate during this century. But this process of expansion, at the Art Institute as at similar institutions around the country, was not achieved without a certain amount of indecision and controversy as the role of the museum in the community changed and architectural ideals were transformed.

Until the beginning of World War I, the Art Institute had found room for expansion primarily by filling in the area enclosed by the wings of the Michigan Avenue, or Allerton, building. The construction of Blackstone Hall in 1903 (see Chronology, p. 10, fig. 10), and the Grand Staircase in 1910 (see Chronology, p. 12, fig. 15) changed the museum from a U-shaped structure into a tightly packed rectangular block.[1] Once this was done, a new direction for expansion was clearly needed.

The logical direction would have been to the north or south along Michigan Avenue. But this raised important legal problems. The lakefront in front of the Loop had been set aside in the earliest days of the city as a "public ground—a common to remain forever open, clear and free of all buildings." Despite pitched battles to erect other public and cultural buildings in the park, only one

institution succeeded in obtaining permission to build a permanent home. In the fever of anticipation that was occasioned by the 1893 World's Fair, the Art Institute was able to obtain the permission of all the adjoining Michigan Avenue property owners and the agreement of the city and the courts to build a museum on park land (see Phipps, pp. 28–45). This agreement stipulated that the new Art Institute could occupy only 400 front-feet along Michigan Avenue.[2]

In the years after the Art Institute built the Allerton Building, the legal situation became more complex. The lakefront strip was greatly expanded by landfill to the east of the Illinois Central Railroad, which had originally run just offshore on a trestle. There was some uncertainty as to whether the old restrictions applied to this new land. In addition, the status of the land changed in 1903, when control of the area was taken over by the South Park Board of Commissioners in order to create a park, now Grant Park.[3]

Because of possible opposition if it tried to build further buildings in the park, the Art Institute chose to move in a different direction in the 1910s. The construction of a bridge (now called Gunsaulus Hall) across the Illinois Central Railroad tracks in 1916 provided for new space that was not over public park land.[4] More importantly, it gave the institution a beachhead on the east side of the tracks, setting the stage for ambitious new expansion plans that would come in the next decade.

The years after the war, particularly the mid-1920s, were expansive ones for the American economy and for its burgeoning art museums. Like many of them, the Art Institute found itself with a rapidly growing collection and too little space to show it. Starting in the late 1920s, the museum began making plans on a huge scale. Apparently, by this time the museum trustees had grown confident that civic pride would sway Michigan Avenue property holders and that they would not block expansion plans. Newspapers carried stories of plans for a 900-foot-long Michigan Avenue facade, and another scheme for the demolition of the existing buildings and the construction of a colossal building that would extend two entire blocks, from Michigan Avenue to the Outer Drive along the lake.[5] At the same time, the museum's director, Robert B. Harshe, was exhorting Chicagoans to use the opportunity presented by the weak economies of Europe to buy as many Old Master paintings as possible in order to cement Chicago's position as one of the world's great art centers.

The museum apparently never released details of any of the plans it was considering, but it did start to build on a small scale (see fig. 2). On the grounds that new construction east of Gunsaulus Hall did not constitute a new building but merely an addition to their existing building and thus did not violate the original agreement with Michigan Avenue property holders, the museum first added the Hutchinson Wing in 1924, which ran along the east edge of the Illinois Central tracks; then McKinlock Court to the east of the Hutchinson Wing in 1924; and galleries south of McKinlock Court in 1924 and 1927. All of these additions were constructed according to designs by the firm of Coolidge and Hodgdon, the successor firm to Shepley, Rutan and Coolidge, designers of the original building.

At the same time, construction was also underway north of McKinlock Court for the museum's theater and the School of the Art Institute. In 1925, the Goodman Theatre auditorium, designed by Howard Van Doren Shaw (1869–1926), a well-known residential architect in Chicago, was built north and east of the new additions. In the late 1920s, a pair of buildings that connected the

FIGURE 2. Aerial view from the east of The Art Institute of Chicago complex, c. 1934. This photograph was included in the program supplied to each of the entrants in the 1934 competition.

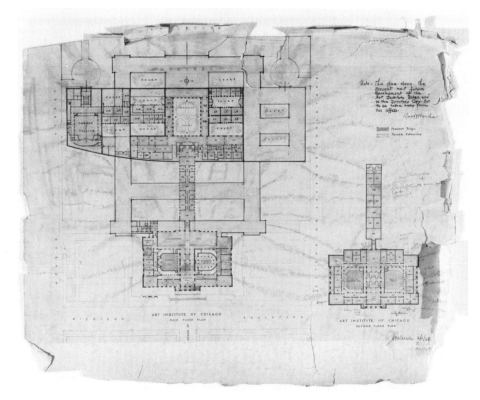

FIGURE 3. Plan of the Art Institute by H. O. Warner, 1928, showing "present and future development" of the complex. This plan was prepared for Art Institute director Robert B. Harshe. The areas outlined without room delineations represent proposed additions, including two new structures spanning the Illinois Central tracks and connected to Gunsaulus Hall.

theater with McKinlock Court was built for the School. For years to come, the space needs of the Goodman Theatre and the School would cause major planning problems.

The configuration of these additions makes it almost certain that they were intended from the beginning as the nucleus of a much larger master plan involving a large, rectangular complex east of the tracks and laid out as a grid of galleries with courtyards between them. Several drawings prepared by the staff of the Art Institute which have been preserved from the late 1920s give some idea of the thinking of museum officials (see fig. 3). Although they differ in a number of ways, these drawings show a series of rectangular galleries, stylistically in keeping with the original building, enclosing a series of courtyards such as the ones that were actually constructed, notably McKinlock Court and the small courts adjacent to it. Of these courtyards, only McKinlock Court itself survives (see Chronology, p. 17, fig. 25). Though it has been altered by the addition in the 1970s of a second story and the blocking of many of the windows looking onto it, it still gives some idea of how the east-wing galleries might have appeared if this plan had been carried out. In these pre-air-conditioned years, the courts would have brought light, air, and a glimpse of nature into the galleries themselves without jeopardizing security. They also would have provided, in good

weather, pleasant places for patrons to rest.

All of this construction was done piece by piece, without great fanfare, while the Art Institute readied itself to make a major expansion. It had applied to the South Park Board and had obtained from them a large amount of land adjoining its existing buildings and filling out a rectangle bounded by Michigan Avenue to the west, Columbus Drive to the east, Jackson Boulevard to the south, and Monroe Street to the north. Confident of success, the museum announced its plans in early 1928, stating that the building committee, composed of Chicago architects David Adler, Jr., John A. Holabird, Art Institute trustee Robert Allerton, and Art Institute attorney Percy B. Eckhart, was considering specifications of the building and that the museum would select an architect through a national competition.[6] Subsequently, the Stevens Hotel on Michigan Avenue brought suit to block the museum from expanding.[7]

Not surprisingly, the stock market crash of 1929 put all plans on hold for a few years. But the prospect of the Art Institute's hosting a giant exhibition of art treasures from across the country during the 1933 Century of Progress Exposition set imaginations racing again.[8] Moreover, fueled by major increases in attendance across the country, a number of art museums were announcing plans for large new buildings or additions to their existing facilities.[9] By 1934, the Art Institute felt ready to embark again on its long-awaited expansion. Coming during the depth of the Depression, the announcement in 1934 that seven of America's most famous architects had been invited to submit plans for major new construction created a considerable stir. The committee responsible for the new building was headed by its chairman, David Adler, Jr., himself a distinguished Chicago architect, with young Louis Skidmore, later to rise to fame with his firm Skidmore, Owings and Merrill, as professional adviser. The jury for the competition included Adler; a number of Chicagoans connected with the Art Institute, including Potter Palmer, Frank G. Logan, John J. Glessner, William O. Goodman, Robert Allerton, and Frederic C. Bartlett; Art Institute director Robert B. Harshe; and Eliel Saarinen, the Finnish architect who was head of the Cranbrook Academy of Fine Arts, the well-known art school outside Detroit.

The museum officials invited an impressive list of architects: Bennett, Parsons and Frost, and Holabird and Root of Chicago; Paul Cret of Philadelphia; and Delano and Aldrich, John Russell Pope, Raymond Hood, and Ralph Walker of New York. The two Chicagoans were very well known. Edward Bennett (1874–1954) had helped Daniel Burnham with the famous 1909 *Plan of Chicago* and was responsible for the design of some of the city's most impressive public commissions, notably the Michigan Avenue Bridge and the Buckingham Fountain. He had also played a leading role in the 1933 Century of Progress fair. John A. Holabird (1886–1945) and John Wellborn Root, Jr. (1887–1963) had built, by the late 1920s, the city's largest and most successful commercial architectural firm, having designed such buildings as the Chicago Board of Trade, the Palmolive (now Playboy) building and the old Daily News building (now Riverside Plaza).

Among the architects from other cities, Paul Cret (1876–1945), a French-born architect living in Philadelphia, had gained a wide reputation already in the 1910s with his winning competition entry for the Pan American Union Building in Washington, D. C. He enjoyed a highly prestigious career as architect and professor at the University of Pennsylvania. William A. Delano (1874–1960) and Chester H. Aldrich (1871–1940) of New York, although they had designed public buildings, including one in 1910 for the Walters Art Gallery in Baltimore, were famous primarily for their elegant houses for the Rockefellers, Whitneys, Astors, and other wealthy East Coast families. Raymond Hood

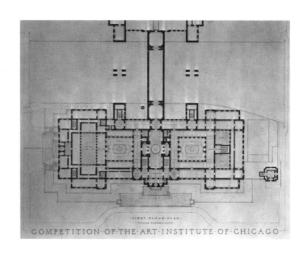

COMPETITION·OF·THE·ART·INSTITUTE·OF·CHICAGO

(1881–1934) and Ralph Walker (1889–1973), on the other hand, were probably the two most important commercial architects in New York in the late 1920s. Early in his career, Hood had been the winner (with his partner John Mead Howells) of the Chicago Tribune Tower competition in 1923. He was the designer of the McGraw Hill and Daily News buildings in New York and the principal force in the creation of Rockefeller Center. Ralph Walker had to his credit several of the most important office buildings in New York, including the dramatic Irving Trust building at the corner of Broadway and Wall Street. Finally, John Russell Pope (1874–1937) had a major reputation for producing meticulously correct designs, often on a grand scale and in a severe classical style, which had earned him the nickname "the last of the Romans." Pope designed a number of public buildings, including the Baltimore Museum of Art, and, shortly after the Art Institute competition, would be given the commission for the most important museum work of this era, the National Gallery in Washington, D. C. Upon the death of Raymond Hood, Ernest Grunsfeld (1897–1970), another Chicago architect and designer of the Michigan Boulevard Garden Apartments and the Adler Planetarium, was added to the list.

In some respects, the firms invited to participate were similar to one another. Each had established itself with a considerable body of work that had been well received. The designers for these firms had enjoyed the best of academic educations; virtually every one of the prin-

FIGURE 4. John Russell Pope (1874–1937). Entry for The Art Institute of Chicago competition, 1934. Original drawing now lost. Pope's was the most classical of all the schemes presented.

cipals had attended the Ecole des Beaux-Arts in Paris. But, although none of these designers could even remotely be considered part of the radical avant-garde that, by the 1930s, had made a major mark in Europe and was represented by a few architects in Chicago, they were far from identical in their point of view and stylistic preferences. While Pope's scholarly, classical compositions might have been considered conservative to the point of being reactionary, Ralph Walker and Holabird and Root represented the most up-to-date architecture in the country for middle-class business clients.

The program statement given to the architects specified that the addition could extend to the north, south, or east of the existing structures, to the museum's property lines east of the Illinois Central tracks, and that the museum had the right to construct four more bridges across the tracks to connect the new addition back to the Michigan Avenue building. The program did not specify what should go into the new wing, but gave the existing amount of square footage for each department and the desired amount of total footage once the addition was constructed, thereby allowing the architects to arrange the entire complex as they judged best.

The program also required that the new addition be designed in such a way that it could be built in stages. There were also certain restrictions about existing structures: the Goodman Theatre auditorium had to be retained, although its exterior could be changed. The retention of McKinlock Court and the reuse of a number of existing foundation walls, on the other hand, were desirable although not obligatory. The only indication given about the actual appearance of the structure was the following: "The building committee urges the competitors to strive for simplicity and character in all of their designs."[10]

The drawings were to be submitted by June 29, 1934. Each contestant was to receive $1,000 for his submission, and the winner would receive the commission for the initial work and $10,000 against his fee.

The proposals received by the Art Institute varied considerably.[11] The most conservative was, not surprisingly, Pope's entry (fig. 4). Pope, whose magnificent design for the National Gallery would constitute the swan song of the strictly correct classical style, produced a composition that consisted of a single, large rectangular block with two large and several smaller interior courts. In using this scheme, Pope was the only one of the entrants who dared to obliterate McKinlock Court. Instead, he placed a great hall at the central east-west axis of his plan and expressed it on the front of the building by a central pedimented entrance pavilion with great arches revealing the elevated main floor. Both the plan and the facade, especially the central feature, recall the original Art Institute building, though on a larger scale. To the sides of the central block were two recessed blocks and, flanking these, two projecting end pavilions which Pope used in an attempt to articulate the enormously long east facade. Across the length of the facade, rows of highly refined rectangular, pedimented window openings added further interest.

The scheme of Delano and Aldrich (fig. 5), though somewhat similar to Pope's plan, maintained McKinlock Court. Low side wings branched off a great rectangle which built up to a pronounced central accent—a high, porticoed central block. Somewhat freer in its classicism than that of Pope, the Delano and Aldrich design was still clearly in the tradition of the great American cultural institutions of the turn of the century.

All of the other entrants chose to use a freer, more stripped-down classicism and relied more on the plan and general proportions of classical buildings than on literal classical details. The entry of Grunsfeld (fig. 6) was perhaps the most unexpected of the set. Long and low, and virtually devoid of architectural or sculptural elements to accentuate the various areas of his elevation, the Grunsfeld scheme seems surprisingly severe and abstract. A little richer in its decorative treatment was the entry by Ralph Walker (fig. 7) in which a giant, unadorned colonnade was framed by two high, projecting blocks that were completely unornamented but had a large alcove for sculpture at the center of each. In both the Grunsfeld and Walker schemes, McKinlock Court was retained as the center of the plan, but screened from view by the new east block.

The other three proposals were fairly similar in both plan and style. Bennett, Parsons and Frost (fig. 8), Paul Cret (fig. 9), and Holabird and Root (fig. 10) all placed their central block to the west, behind McKinlock Court, and enclosed the court on the north and south with projecting wings, making it into a forecourt for their compositions. Where the Holabird and Root and Paul Cret schemes built up from the lower side wings to a higher central portion, the Bennett, Parsons and Frost scheme was kept low, apparently in an attempt to allow the viewer to see the original Art Institute building and the pediment of Gunsaulus Hall behind it. All were in the heavy, severe style that characterized much of monumental architecture throughout the western world in the 1930s. Of all of the schemes, that of Holabird and Root, with its long horizontal bands of windows and wide bands of flat masonry, was probably considered by most observers as the most stylistically advanced of the lot.

On July 18, 1934, the major Chicago papers all ran prominent stories announcing that Holabird and Root had been named winners of the competition. The papers characterized the winning entry as completely up-to-

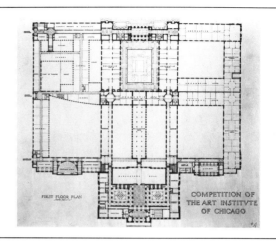

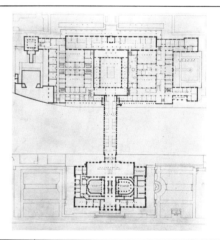

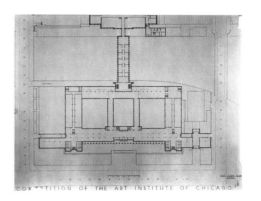

62

FIGURE 5. William A. Delano (1874–1960) and Chester H. Aldrich (1871–1940). Entry for
The Art Institute of Chicago competition, 1934. Original drawing now lost.

FIGURE 6. Ernest Grunsfeld (1897–1970). Entry for The Art Institute of Chicago
competition, 1934. Original drawing now lost. Grunsfeld's entry was unexpectedly severe
and abstract.

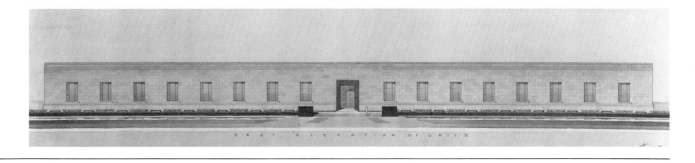

FIGURE 7. Ralph Walker (1889–1973). Entry for The Art Institute of Chicago competition,
1934. Original drawing now lost.

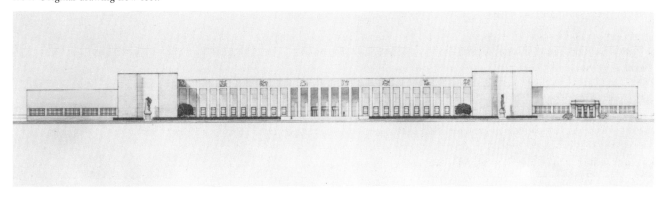

FIGURE 8. Bennett, Parsons and Frost, architects. Entry for The Art Institute of Chicago competition, 1934. Original drawing now lost. The architects of this scheme kept the building low so that the rooflines of the original building and the pediment of Gunsaulus Hall could be seen.

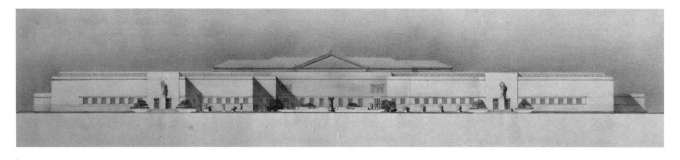

FIGURE 9. Paul Cret (1876–1945). Entry for The Art Institute of Chicago competition, 1934. Original drawing now lost.

FIGURE 10. John A. Holabird (1886–1945) and John Wellborn Root, Jr. (1887–1963). Winning entry for The Art Institute of Chicago competition, 1934. Holabird and Root's entry was considered the most stylistically and technically up-to-date of the group.

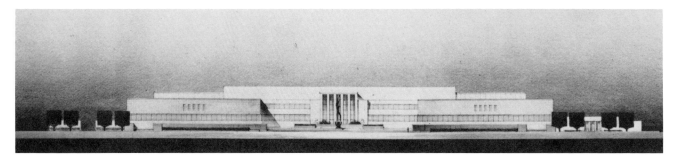

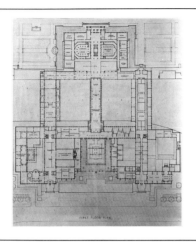

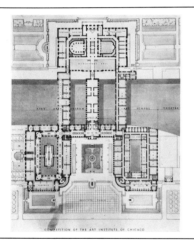

date in appearance and equipment. The articles described the specially designed moveable panels that were to be used in changing the configurations of the large, open gallery spaces; the complete air-conditioning scheme; the escalators to an underground garage; and, perhaps the most striking feature of the entire scheme, the system of lighting. Skylights had been traditional since the turn of the century, but here they were abandoned in favor of wall windows. This system, which represented a sharp departure from the prevailing practice, would be further worked out by Holabird and Root with the help of a small, experimental building—essentially a moving room—that they designed to run on tracks south of Goodman Theatre in order to provide different lighting conditions.[12]

The two runners-up were the other two Chicago firms. Although the entries were delivered anonymously, with the name of the architect in a sealed envelope that was to be opened only after the jury had reached its decision, the fact that the three winners were Chicagoans, and that John Holabird had been a trustee of the Art Institute since 1925, resigning in 1934 to enter the competition, and had also been a member of the building committee that had inaugurated the competition, might seem like a conflict of interest to many observers today, but, at the time, it was not considered unusual and little was made of it.[13]

The intention of the museum trustees was to build the complex, whose cost was estimated at $9,000,000, over the next ten or twenty years. Immediately, however, they intended to proceed with the first unit of the building,

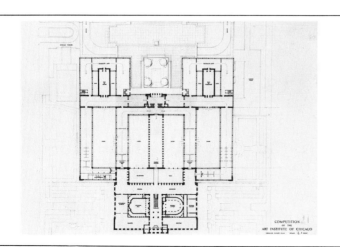

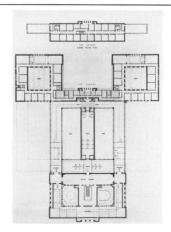

FIGURE 11. Holabird and Root and Burgee, architects.
Perspective rendering of proposed B. F. Ferguson Memorial
Building, c. 1955.

which the architects had designated on the drawings as
"Unit A" and which was apparently to be located directly over the existing Hutchinson Gallery. It was to be
built at a cost of no more than $600,000.[14]

The subsequent history of this project was an unhappy one. Newspapers reported that the first unit
would be financed by money from the B. F. Ferguson
Fund. This fund, established in 1905, was designated for
use in commissioning public monuments in Chicago.
Artists and others in Chicago were outraged that the Art
Institute, which manages the fund, would deprive the
city of sculpture and artists of commissions so that the
museum trustees could use it for a building. The Art
Institute went to the courts in what turned out to be a
successful bid for this use of the fund, but the decision
led to further controversies between area artists and the
museum.[15]

But even with the Ferguson Fund money in hand, the
museum decided to back away from its plans to start
construction. At their May 1935 meeting, the trustees
decided to delay construction pending the acquisition of
further funding.[16] In 1937, the director reported that

$200,000 was still needed to proceed with the first unit.
In 1939, the Allerton Wing, a new set of galleries for
decorative arts, was added to the south of McKinlock
Court. The wing was erected according to designs of
Holabird and Root but not, it appears, in accord with
their overall scheme, even though a new model for the
entire complex had been published during 1938.[17] By
this time, war was again on the horizon and the Art
Institute was once again forced to shelve expansion
plans. "Unit A" was still on the drawing boards at the
Holabird office as late as 1958, but by then Holabird and
Root had become Holabird and Root and Burgee, and
the firm was already working on a new Art Institute
expansion program on the Michigan Avenue side of the
complex.

II. The Postwar Building Campaigns

At the end of the Korean War, the Art Institute still
found itself in basically the same quarters it had occupied in the 1920s, and with severe problems in its
existing plant.[18] The museum had, since the mid-1930s,
plans in hand for its vast new complex east of the Illinois
Central Railroad tracks. But, when work actually
started, it was not to the east of the tracks but rather to
the north and to the south of the original building. By

the time this phase was finished, the original building was flanked on the north and south sides with a new wing and a new garden in front of each. These additions created controversy for the museum, but they helped ease the space shortage at the Art Institute and today bear interesting testimony to the changing ideals of museum architecture during the postwar years.

B.F. Ferguson Memorial Building

The exact reasons for the failure of the Art Institute in the 1950s to build the new East Wing designed by Holabird and Root for the 1934 competition are not clear. It does not appear that the problem lay with the design, since both the museum and the architects still expected to go forward with this scheme as late as the late 1950s. In the meantime, construction of new administrative quarters, anticipated since the late 1920s, apparently came to be a higher priority.[19] By 1954, the trustees had decided to shift the use of the interest accrued in the Ferguson Fund, which now totaled some $1.2 million, from the East Wing to the proposed administrative structure which would lie north of their main building. The trustees went back to the courts for approval and, at their meeting of October 11, 1954, the trustees accepted the proposal of Holabird and Root and Burgee to design the building, charging the Art Institute only out-of-pocket expenses.

The program for the new structure was approved on April 20, 1955, at which time John Root, in the absence of his partner John Holabird (who had died in 1945), presented drawings (see figs. 11, 12; see also Chronology, p. 18, fig. 26). He stipulated that the new building was to be made of the same materials as the existing building and artificially weathered to conform in texture and color. Along with the new wing, the plans called for renovating some of the space in the original building for exhibition space when offices were moved to the new wing, for remodeling Blackstone Hall, and for building a new heating plant.[20]

Plans were ninety-five percent complete by June 1955, but work was halted for an indefinite period when it was learned that the use of the Ferguson Fund money had been challenged in the courts by the City of Chicago, the National Sculptors Society, and Artists Equity. All of these groups had the same objections that had surfaced in the 1930s. They argued that using the money for

a building violated Ferguson's intention in creating the fund to provide sculptural monuments for the city. The bitter fight dragged on in the courts for over a year, but, in June 1956, Circuit Judge Charles S. Doughtery approved the use of some $1.2 million of fund moneys to construct the new wing, arguing that the building would be a fitting memorial to Ferguson.[21]

The continuing friction with the city and its artists was not the end of the Art Institute's problems. When the bids for the building came in early in 1957, they were higher than anticipated, but construction went forward anyway.[22] The opening of the new wing in November 1958 was clouded by news that the Art Institute had run into financial troubles and that its director, Daniel Catton Rich, had abruptly resigned.[23]

The problem that had confronted Helmuth Bartsch, the designer at Holabird and Root and Burgee who was in charge of the building, was clearly a daunting one.[24] The original building had been designed as a single, free-standing unit. The addition of a wing to one side of such a forceful, self-contained classical building was a perfect example of a design problem that has perplexed architects since antiquity. It was important that an addition be sympathetic to the existing building, but in these years, when European modernist architecture was starting to have a major impact on American practice, the con-

FIGURE 12. Holabird and Root and Burgee. Detail of model of the Art Institute (see fig. 13), showing proposed Ferguson Building, c. 1958.

tinued use of specific stylistic features of the late nineteenth century would have been considered unacceptably old-fashioned.

The new wing also had to look as if it were the left-hand wing of what would eventually be a three-part composition. This suggested a certain amount of asymmetry in the new work so that it would deflect toward the main building and balance a similar asymmetrical treatment on the other side. There are, in fact, drawings and models by the architects, apparently made for presentation to the trustees, that show what the museum would have looked like with a virtual mirror image of their new building, presumably for exhibition space, to the south of the main building (see fig. 13). But because the Ferguson Wing was to be set well back from the street and was itself so large, it needed to look complete and balanced on its own. The program for offices, furthermore, was very different from that for galleries and created a further problem. Where the main building was treated as a single, high story set on a raised basement, an arrangement that accorded perfectly with the high

FIGURE 13. Model of the Art Institute showing proposed Ferguson Building to the north (left) and symmetrical addition to the south (right). The original proposal called for the new structures to be identical, but the commission for the south addition was awarded to another architect (see fig. 16).

gallery spaces within, the administrative building, because of its lower ceiling heights, would house several floors for each level of the old building. This in turn required a completely different window pattern than the one used in the main building.

Bartsch's severe, rectangular box is one of the most complex and mannered compositions of this period to be found anywhere (see fig. 14). He clearly wanted to relate his building to the classical tradition as seen in the original building. But the new wing is more directly indebted to the kind of stripped, monumental manner used by many architects in the United States and elsewhere from the 1920s until well after World War II, a tradition that was also seen in his firm's own 1934 competition scheme. It was meant to be severely grand, and the exteriors were carried out with great care in the same durable materials as the main block. In order to give the new wing sufficient weight and solidity and, probably, to balance the long stretches of unbroken wall which were anticipated on the south wing (museum practice had turned away from the use of natural light and toward artificial illumination of works of art), they opened the Michigan Avenue facade with a single door and only three ranks of small windows.

But the architects obviously felt that they had to make the building modern as well. The treatment of the stone facing is deliberately thin, making clear that it is a mere

FIGURE 14. View from the west of the north Stanley McCormick Memorial Court as it was landscaped in 1960.

veneer over a steel frame rather than the supporting material of the wall itself. The windows, square in shape rather than the high rectangles used in classical architecture, were punched through the wall without frames. Still, the reading of the windows as modern elements is equivocal. Some indication of a traditional window frame is implied by the use of narrow, horizontal bands of facing stone which run above and below every window. These bands, which articulate the whole facade by their rhythmic alternation with wider bands, divide the facade the way string courses do on classical buildings, but their flatness and spacing gives the facade a tension more in keeping with the modernism of the 1950s than with the feel of the original building.

The monumental door, likewise, maintains a constant tension between the classic and the modern. The massive door itself is paneled in bronze as though it were the main portal to a cathedral or palace, but the panels are completely flat and the obvious solidity of the door is contrasted with a band of clear glass running all around it, instead of a heavy masonry frame, suggesting once again the fact that this is a modern steel-frame building rather than a classical masonry one. The doorway is raised above the terrace level by a set of three granite steps, and the entire opening is edged with a similar granite, creating a degree of monumentality. But the placement of the doorway, not in the center of the building or on any axis, but under the last rank of windows

(now filled in), undercuts its grandeur. At the top of the building something resembling a cornice was made by cutting a narrow channel in the stone near the top of the wall; but the narrowness of this channel, and the fact that the upper portion of the wall does not protrude beyond the lower wall, complete the ambiguity between the monumental classicality and the thinner, more tenuous modernity that runs throughout the facade.

The wonderfully mannered subtleties of the finished building were lost on both the architectural avant-garde, which roundly condemned the building for being old-fashioned, and a considerable group of people, many of them closely connected with the Art Institute, who would have preferred something more canonically classic. In fact, within a year, there was talk within the institution about altering it. Mrs. Stanley McCormick, who proposed donating a garden to go in front of the building, was clearly unhappy. At her urging, the building committee authorized the replacement of the modern balustrades in front of the Ferguson Wing with ones that matched the original building.[25] They explored the possibility of removing the windows in the building and reworking the cornice so that it would match the Morton Wing which was by then under construction to the south.[26] These alterations were delayed because of concern about the legal and professional ethics involved with altering the work of Holabird and Root and Burgee, and, in the end, no action was taken.[27]

Stanley McCormick Memorial Court (North Garden)

In their drawings for the Ferguson Wing, the architects had given some indications of the kind of garden that might go in front of it (see fig. 11). On January 3, 1959, the Chicago newspapers announced that Mrs. Stanley McCormick, widow of Stanley McCormick, had given a substantial gift to create such a garden in honor of her late husband.[28] A drawing published in the paper showed a set of planters containing trees and bushes that, according to the announcement, were selected to retain their contours in winter months and to give maximum shade in summer. The garden plan had an asymmetrical composition, with the main axis running past a large pool with three jets of water in it, up a monumental stairway to a platform just in front of the Ferguson Wing on which there were to be three monumental flagpoles with sculptural bases. According to the article, the pavement was to be precast concrete slabs filled with marble chips forming a pattern in gray and green and separated from the planted areas with borders of pink granite. A retaining wall of the same materials was to run along Monroe Street.

Although the final design was similar to the schemes suggested by Holabird and Root and Burgee during the design of the Ferguson Wing, and although it was done in their offices, knowledgeable sources suggest that Mrs. McCormick had insisted that the final arrangements be carried out by her own landscape designer.[29] Work was begun in March 1959 and finished early in 1960.[30] Somewhat later, the three bronze flagpoles, procured in Europe, were added.[31] The blue mosaic tiles in the fountain basin proved to be a problem and they were eventually covered over. There was also talk about replacing the existing fountains with a sculptural group from Paris, but this effort was never successful.[32]

The finished garden design (fig. 14) shares many of the same characteristics as the Ferguson Building. It seems to take as a starting point a classical tradition, with its use of symmetrical geometric forms, here created by rows of hawthorne trees and beds of flowers defined by forsythia hedges, and to make it asymmetrical and more abstract. Perhaps the most remarkable feature is the architectonic way in which the plant material is treated, especially the trimmed hedges, to create roomlike areas which enclose trees placed in dynamically asymmetrical positions. The garden has a severity similar to that of the building, and the same kind of balanced but asymmetrical composition that extends down to the pattern of wide and narrow granite blocks in a syncopated pattern

FIGURE 15. Holabird and Root and Burgee. Plan of proposed Art Institute additions and gardens, c. 1958.

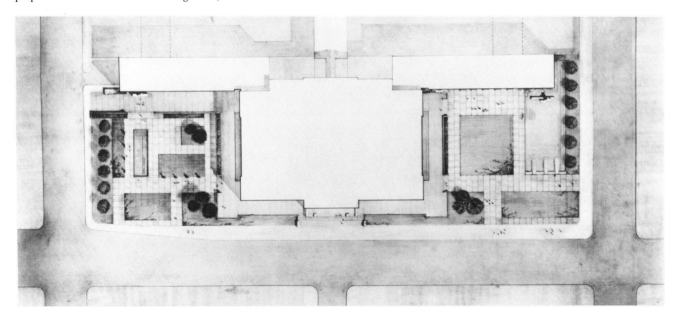

70

FIGURE 16. Alfred Shaw of Shaw, Metz and Associates, architects. Elevation of Morton Wing and proposed garden, c. 1962.

along the retaining wall east of the garden. Carefully planted and well maintained, the garden softens considerably the lines of the Ferguson Wing and helps ease the transition with the main building.

The Morton Wing

By the end of 1959, the Art Institute had reorganized its leadership, dividing what had been the director's job between two positions, an administrative director and a fine-arts director. The new administrative director, Allen McNab, was thus free to concentrate on the building program and to proceed with the construction of a new wing to the south of the main building and the garden in front of it (see fig. 15).[33] In the meantime, a fund drive that had been launched to ease the museum's financial burdens had succeeded in bringing in badly needed new funds. In a meeting of the Committee on Buildings and Grounds on December 9, 1959, architect Alfred Shaw presented designs for the new Morton Wing, named for Sterling Morton, a Chicago business and civic leader who had left the museum $1.2 million for the new structure in his will.[34] It is not clear why the museum bypassed Holabird and Root and Burgee, who had done much of the museum's design work since the 1930s and who might have been expected to create the southern pendant to their building to the north. But the experience of the Ferguson Wing had not been a pleasant one, and the committee turned instead to Alfred Shaw of Shaw, Metz and Associates. Shaw was an architect of the same generation as John Root, and, like Root, had been

an important designer already in the 1920s and 1930s. Although Shaw had worked for Graham, Anderson, Probst and White, a conservative firm, his Field Building at 135 South LaSalle Street in Chicago was the last and most severe of all the high office buildings designed before the stock market crash. In the following years, Shaw's office was responsible for a number of buildings that, while not abandoning altogether the classical tradition, pushed it almost to the point of unrecognizability by the use of modernist motifs and materials.[35]

For the Morton Wing (fig. 16; see also Chronology, p. 20, fig. 30), which would sit on the existing foundations of a low classroom structure erected in 1910, Shaw took a very different approach from that taken by Holabird and Root and Burgee. The main feature of his building consisted of a single, windowless stone-faced block ornamented only with a highly abstracted cornice at the top and a single inscription in carefully cut classical letters. He proposed to move in front of this block the Fountain of the Great Lakes by Lorado Taft, which since its erection in 1913 had sat just south of the main building (in what would become the north edge of the Morton Wing garden). This part of his building, which recalls in a number of ways John Russell Pope's National Gallery in Washington, D.C., was perhaps more conservative than that of Holabird and Root and Burgee, but the solid masonry part of the wing was connected to the main building by a passageway clad in a frankly modern steel-and-glass curtain wall through which viewers could see a dramatic, freestanding helical stairway leading from the lower to the upper gallery level (see figs. 17, 18). This

FIGURE 17. View from the east of the spiral staircase and west window in the Morton Wing, c. 1960. The steel-and-glass window wall provides a frankly modern link between the old and new buildings.

FIGURE 18. View from the north of the second-floor galleries in the Morton Wing, c. 1960. At right is the gracefully curved balustrade at the top of the spiral staircase.

engineering tour de force, a dramatically narrow ribbon of monolithic reinforced concrete, was placed in the passage like a giant piece of sculpture, and it constituted the chief ornament of the wing.[36] The lower floor of the main block of the building was to house temporary exhibitions, and the upper level would house contemporary American artists.

As soon as these plans were announced, old controversies were rekindled. Along with the usual complaints that the museum was becoming too large a presence in Grant Park, many Chicagoans felt that the fountain should not be moved and that, if a new piece of sculpture was needed for the new wing, it should be newly commissioned.[37] But, by March 1961, plans for the new wing had been approved by the Park District. Despite some problems with construction, notably the difficulties of placing foundations for the sculpture over an underground garage, the building opened in October 1962 with an exhibition called "Treasures of Versailles" in the ground-floor galleries.

On hand for the opening was a small group of picketers carrying signs that read "Chicago Needs Fountains" and "Ferguson's Millions Buy Ugly Buildings," the latter apparently in the mistaken belief that both the north and south wings had been constructed with Ferguson Fund money. Otherwise, the opening appears to have inspired very little comment, negative or positive, in the press about the building's appearance. This was probably due in part to simple exhaustion after such a long and complicated building campaign. It was also surely due to the fact that the Morton Wing reflected the taste of conservative individuals, including many museum visitors. The use of the curtain wall to link the old building with the new was probably inspired in part by postwar notions about preservation and conservation in which it was considered important to distinguish quite clearly between old work and new. The monumental stone block, with its cool classical poise (which nevertheless rejected specific classical motifs), was also an approved method for dealing with a problem like that of adding to a grand structure such as the Art Institute's main building. Since Shaw's nearly contemporary work at the Chicago Historical Society was buried in early 1988 under new construction, this building represents one of the best remaining examples of the very last gasp of the unornamented, monumental, classical tradition that flowered in the 1930s and all but vanished after the 1960s.

South Stanley McCormick Memorial Court

The one portion of the expansion campaign of the 1950s and 1960s that seems to have elicited almost universal praise was the south Stanley McCormick Memorial Court, the garden in front of the Morton Wing (see figs. 19, 20). Opened on Memorial Day 1965, it was again the gift of Mrs. Stanley McCormick.[38] The work of landscape architect Dan Kiley, with Harry Weese and Associates as local architects, this garden responds admirably to its site and to the buildings around it, but, curiously enough, it was not the plan that the designer had wished to see executed.

According to Pat Shaw, Kiley was suggested by his father, Alfred Shaw. Kiley, working out of Charlotte, Vermont, was already a well-known landscape architect, having completed landscape designs for numerous corporate headquarters, the United States Air Force Academy, Dulles Airport near Washington, D.C., and Lincoln Center in New York City.[39] His initial idea was to create a water garden, inspired in part by the gardens of Mughal India and Moorish Spain. He mentions as one of his most important sources the Court of the Orange

FIGURE 19. View from the west of the south Stanley McCormick Memorial Court as it was built in 1965. The garden was designed by Dan Kiley, the landscape architect known for his work in Columbus, Indiana, at the John F. Kennedy Memorial Library in Boston, and at the Ford Foundation in New York City. Photo: Aaron Kiley.

Trees in the Giralda at Seville, in which trees were set twenty feet apart with an irrigation network running through them, creating a kind of fret-work pattern of water and foliage.[40] According to Kiley, his initial scheme for the garden was one of the first of his geometric water gardens, and would lead to important later works, notably his spectacular Fountain Place in Dallas.

Kiley apparently had to follow the elderly Mrs. McCormick around the country from Chicago to New York to her house in Santa Barbara, California, in order to get approval. When he finally reached her, Mrs. McCormick vetoed the idea of the water garden. Instead, Kiley proposed, and used, a series of hawthorne trees in planters on beds of gravel, with a single pool in the center (see fig. 20). His idea was for the trees to be clipped so that they came together overhead in a series of

FIGURE 20. View from the southeast of the south Stanley McCormick Memorial Court. Photo: Aaron Kiley.

arches that were meant to complement the simple, solid masonry wall of Morton Wing to the east and the more elaborate arched south facade of the main Art Institute building to the north. In the axis centering on the Taft fountain that had recently been reinstalled in the center of the Morton Wing facade, Kiley placed a large pool (see fig. 19).

By the end of this building campaign, the Art Institute presented to Michigan Avenue a continuous facade stretching two full blocks from Jackson Boulevard on the south to Monroe Street on the north. After several decades, most of the controversy that surrounded the buildings has been forgotten. Although both of the wings still look a little uneasy in their attempt to combine classical monumentality with modern expression, the fact that all of the parts were faced with the same material, had an even cornice line, and were tied together by a continuous balustrade gives the composition a certain amount of unity and consistency. In fact, it appears likely that recent events in the architectural world will make it possible to appreciate these buildings more than ever before.[41] Certainly the well-maintained, landscaped gardens in front of the wings, in addition to providing a welcome oasis in the city, also help in setting off admirably the main building. Despite differences in construction dates and in the styles of the individual buildings, the ensemble possesses a unity and serenity that would be the envy of most urban museums.

III. The East Wing Additions

For a number of months during the late 1960s and early 1970s, there was no construction anywhere on the Art Institute's buildings or grounds. In part, this reflected a period of consolidation in the museum. It also reflected the turbulent era of the late 1960s in which the country's art museums, along with most of its established institutions, came under attack by students and others as elitist defenders of the social and political status quo.[42] But it soon became apparent that this period constituted only a brief pause before the museum launched into its biggest building campaign yet—the construction of a vast new East Wing. This project precipitated a rethinking of the planning ideas that had guided the Art Institute since the 1920s, and pushed the institution into a new era of architectural design.

After completion of the Morton Wing, the pace of construction slowed noticeably. The south McCormick Court was not completed until 1965. Existing spaces were remodeled to create the Junior Museum, which opened in 1964; the A. Montgomery Ward Gallery, which opened in 1967; and the Architecture Gallery, which also opened in 1967 (see Chronology, p. 20). Discussions about long-range needs were underway, however, and in 1970 the museum announced in its *Annual Report* that the architectural firm of Skidmore, Owings and Merrill (SOM) had been retained to survey the needs of the museum and its schools. In conjunction with this announcement, the trustees revealed that they had decided to embark on a $50 million fund-raising effort whose completion would coincide with the institution's one-hundreth anniversary in 1979, and that they were in the last stages of negotiations with the Illinois Central Railroad to obtain permission to build new bridges over the tracks parallel to Gunsaulus Hall.[43]

The selection of Skidmore, Owings and Merrill clearly indicated that the museum had decided to abandon the plans for the east wing which Holabird and Root had drawn up in the 1930s and which had been revised from time to time through the late 1950s. It also meant that the museum administration reached a turning point in its ideas about architectural design, and that the trustees were ready to abandon the classical tradition that had guided all designs since the opening of the original building in the 1890s. Unlike the firm of Holabird and Root, which traced its origins back to the 1880s, or of Shaw and Associates, which could trace a lineage back to Daniel Burnham's firm, SOM had been founded in the 1930s and had made its reputation in the 1950s with relentlessly modernist designs, such as the gleaming stainless-steel-and-plate-glass Inland Steel Building. The vice-president of Inland Steel, not coincidentally, was Leigh Block, who was president of the Art Institute's Board of Trustees from 1970 to 1975. By 1970, SOM had become the city's largest and best-known architectural office for major commercial work. The firm's partners were well known to the businessmen on the Art Institute's Board of Trustees, and several of the partners, notably William Hartmann, collected art and were active in Art Institute affairs. The decision to hire SOM was, like the decisions to hire all the Art Institute's previous architects, based on a close association that had been built up between the Art Institute and the firm.

The choice of partner Walter Netsch to design the new wing was also logical. Netsch had established a reputation as a designer for academic and cultural institutions, having made his name in the 1950s with the Air Force Academy in Colorado Springs. He went on to do buildings for many institutions, including the Chicago campus of the University of Illinois and libraries for the University of Chicago and Northwestern University. By the 1970s, he had come to be closely associated with his controversial "Field Theory," a method of designing based on the rotation of geometric forms. Netsch had also amassed a considerable collection of modern art.[44]

The museum itself came under new management at just this moment. In 1972, E. Laurence Chalmers, Jr., was appointed as president to replace Charles Cunningham, and there was a major shakeup in the institution's organization. Where Cunningham was a Harvard-trained art historian, Chalmers was a psychologist and university administrator with no previous background in art. What the trustees were apparently seeking, among other things, was a man who could bring to the museums the kind of organizational and fund-raising skills needed to get their enormous expansion built.[45] Soon thereafter, Leigh Block was named president of the Board of Trustees.

The problems facing the architects were prodigious. The museum had, like many large institutions, grown piece by piece over the years as budget and space needs dictated. There had been master plans at least since the 1920s, but none of these plans had been followed for very long before some new set of circumstances or change in aesthetic idea had rendered them obsolete. Many casual visitors, as well as the museum's staff members, found large parts of the complex confusing and inconvenient, especially in those areas where the intermingling of galleries, public spaces, and School facilities led to difficulties in function, circulation, and security. Certainly the most immediately pressing problem was that of the School, which had long been shunted from one part of the complex to another, and which recently had been obliged to rent at considerable expense a large amount of space at 208 South Wabash Avenue.

Because of the painful memories of past criticism of the museum's expansions in Grant Park and use of the Ferguson Fund money, and due to the strident criticisms leveled at museums in general in the late 1960s, there was some reluctance to build a huge new building. The architects considered several alternatives. Two of these involved schemes in which the museum would not expand its current site at all. In the first, reasoning that the museum should reach out into the neighborhoods, the architects explored expansion through the use of mobile programs or branches, bringing art to a public that didn't or couldn't often travel to Chicago's Loop. This solution, however, created tremendous logistical problems in the transportation of objects, high insurance costs, and security. The second possibility was to remain within the existing complex, but to contract the space devoted to peripheral activities, cafeterias, bookstores, and the like in order to provide more room for modern

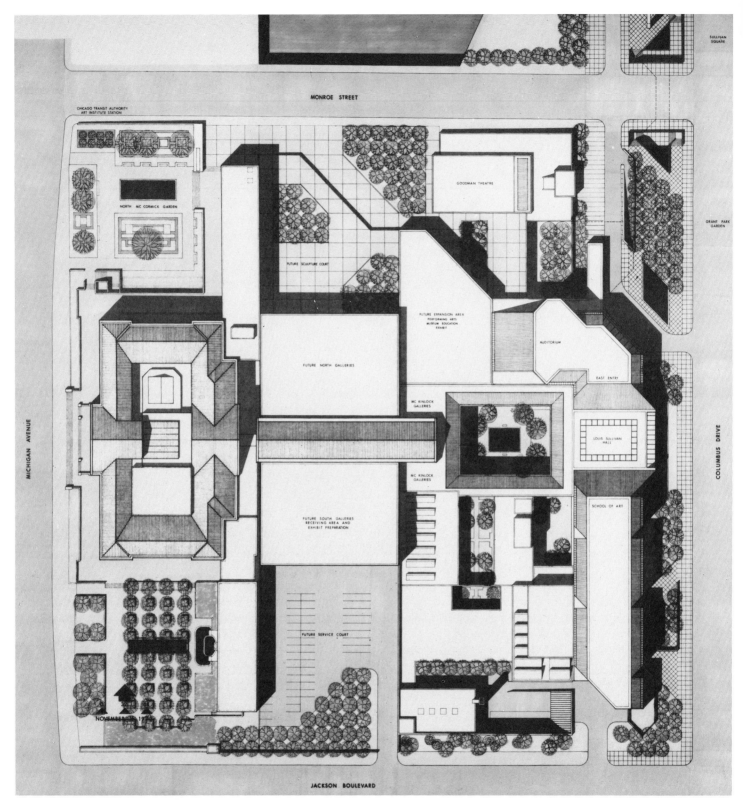

FIGURE 21. Walter Netsch of Skidmore, Owings and Merrill, architects. "Ultimate Master Plan" for The Art Institute of Chicago, c. 1971. This proposal called for the Illinois Central Railroad tracks to be replaced by courtyards, for additions on the north and south of Gunsaulus Hall, and a tunnel to a parking garage on Monroe Street. Ink and wash on paper; 102.9 × 101.6 cm.

storage and study areas. But in the end, the architects and museum officials decided that their obligation was to the public as well as to scholars and that their only course was to expand greatly the physical plant in order to satisfy the increased space needs of all the various departments. This meant expansion to the east of the Illinois Central Railroad tracks into Grant Park.[46]

In November 1971, the museum announced the results of this study. The architects recommended a two-phase plan for future expansion that would include refurbishing the existing galleries and creating new space for the Prints and Photographs Department (as it was called then), and, east of the Illinois Central tracks, adding a new wing, an outdoor sculpture court, an auditorium, and a School building (see figs. 21–26; see also Chronology, pp. 20–21, figs. 32, 33). These structures were to be built over and around existing Art Institute buildings and into what was a rather bleak expanse along Columbus Avenue of parking for the museum and the Goodman Theatre. The museum agreed to reimburse the Park District for the additional land it would occupy. The Park District in turn planned to more than replace the number of parking spaces in a new garage located under the park just north of Monroe Street. The museum's scheme would bring together all of the School activities under one roof adjacent to, but not in, the museum complex; centralize many of the museum's public functions, such as the dining areas, auditorium, and the board rooms, in one place that could be accessible without opening the galleries; provide vastly improved loading and service areas; and, eventually, add greatly to the museum's gallery space.

The plans for the first phase of the expansion were announced in December 1972 and included the completion of an air-conditioning system for the entire museum; the remodeling of the Print and Drawing Department; and the creation of new galleries around the existing McKinlock Court; a new four-level School building; a new members' lounge and restaurant; and a new, 1,000-seat auditorium. This phase would include most of the public functions of the institution. The second phase would fill in the remaining areas east of the tracks and cover over the Illinois Central tracks with more galleries and paved courts. The first phase was to cost $46 million and was to be completed by 1979.[47] The museum issued a handsome booklet, "The Art Institute of Chicago: The Bold and the Prudent" which outlined the history of the complex and published drawings illustrating the proposed new construction.

FIGURE 22. View from the north of the Columbus Drive entrance. To the right is the entrance to the Goodman Theatre.

The planners had to come to grips with several important issues.[48] One was the matter of building over the railroad. Although museum officials thought they were near an agreement with the Illinois Central Railroad, the possible construction of a subway from McCormick Place, south of the Loop, along the Illinois Central right-of-way through the Art Institute site, to the John Hancock Center on North Michigan Avenue, delayed these negotiations. Partly because of this uncertainty, all of the construction over the tracks, including proposed galleries immediately north and south of Gunsaulus Hall, a sculpture court facing on Monroe Street, and a service court on Jackson Boulevard were relegated to the second phase of the expansion.[49]

Another problem was the question of the permanence of the museum's affiliation with the School of the Art Institute, the Goodman Theatre, and the School of Drama. In the earliest schemes, it appears that the architects had proposed a new theater complex on the northeast corner of the Art Institute block that would have balanced the new School building to the south. But it was apparent that the trustees were already considering ways to divest themselves of the Goodman Theatre and the School of Drama, and there was also considerable sentiment for preserving the interior of the existing theater, which had been designed by Howard Van Doren Shaw.[50] The architects responded by leaving the theater area intact but placing a colonnade in front of the low theater buildings in order to tie them visually to the rest of the new wing (see fig. 22); and creating a new large sign visible from Michigan Avenue.

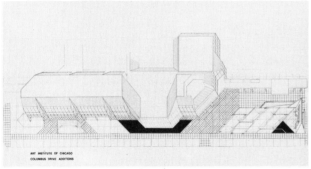

FIGURE 23. Walter Netsch of Skidmore, Owings and Merrill. Model of the Art Institute East Wing (now The Arthur Rubloff Building) and School additions, c. 1971.

FIGURE 24. Walter Netsch of Skidmore, Owings and Merrill. Axonometric drawing of the East Wing and School additions, c. 1971.

Although the Art Institute was committed to the School, which was conceived of as an integral part of the institution, doubts remained in the minds of many, and the architects were instructed to create classroom areas that could be turned into galleries if necessary. The result was a series of largely unfenestrated, loftlike spaces illuminated with narrow, triangular pieces of window-wall carved out of the main block and "light wells" that allowed natural light entry into the partially sunken lower level. This brought natural light into the interior without opening up large windows that might become a problem if the building reverted to gallery space. These notches also broke up somewhat the large bulk of the building, which Netsch also rendered less massive by beveling back the top of the facade (see figs. 23, 24).

Certainly one of the most delicate parts of the new scheme would be the relation of the old building to the new. Netsch states that he tried to be contextual in his responses, keeping the new buildings long and low, for example, and cladding them with limestone (see fig. 25). But Netsch went much further than any of his predecessors in creating a building that broke with the classical tradition. Resolutely modern in its avoidance of applied ornament or specific historical details, it was highly asymmetrical rather than axial and symmetrical; and, because it was created as a "Field Theory" building, it was filled with forty-five-degree diagonals rather than the strictly rectilinear lines of the old building.

Nowhere was the problem of relating new to old more critical than in the area of McKinlock Court. It appears that one of the schemes considered early in the design process would have involved putting a glass roof over McKinlock Court and removing the Carl Milles sculpture (see Chronology, p. 17, fig. 25) to the east entrance.[51] Because of the enormous affection for this outdoor space on the part of the public and the Art Institute staff, it was finally agreed to leave the court open and merely add a second story around it. This second story would provide more gallery space, and it would also ease the circulation problems created by the fact that McKinlock Court was built at a level considerably lower than the rest of the museum. With the creation of this second level of galleries, it became possible for the first time to walk through the entire complex essentially on one level. Although they did not use any of the stylistic elements from the existing McKinlock Court building, in order to maintain as much as possible the feel of the older buildings around the court, the architects chose to place their second-story galleries well back from the wall plane, allowing the original rooftop balustrade to remain intact. They also angled the roof sharply down to the courtyard so that it intruded visually as little as possible. According to Netsch, "New openings on the second level will be proportional to the bays of the original architecture, details will be similar and the intimate scale will be retained."[52] The east facade of Gunsaulus Hall was maintained and was originally intended to be visible inside the second-story addition through the windows at the west end of the courtyard.[53]

A final problem was the matter of the incorporation of elements from the Chicago Stock Exchange Building. Following the announcement that this important building by Adler and Sullivan was to be demolished, preservation and other citizen groups mounted a major campaign to try to rescue the building. These efforts culminated in a flurry of last-minute activity in late 1971, just as plans for the new Art Institute wing were being drawn up. The efforts to save the structure were futile, however. The final legal roadblock to demolition was cleared in October 1971 and demolition began shortly thereafter.[54] In the meantime, The Metropolitan Museum of Art in New York City proposed to acquire the arched entryway and the surrounding bays of the building's exterior and move them to New York for reinstallation in their American wing courtyard.[55] Apparently stung by widespread criticism for allowing the building to be demolished and by the Metropolitan's proposal, Mayor Richard Daley intervened to keep the entrance arch and much of the decorative work in Chicago. The entrance arch was finally donated to the city.[56] At the same time, the Art Institute started planning ways to incorporate as much of the ornamental detail as possible in the projected new wing. The most spectacular space in the old building had been the Trading Room, but it had long ago been remodeled out of recognition. The museum hired architects John Vinci and David Kenny, and photographer Richard Nickel, to uncover what remained of the room, to record it, and to salvage key elements while the building was being demolished.[57] These elements included one ceiling bay with its original stenciled designs, two of the four original capitals, some plaster ornament, and most of the skylight mullions and art glass. In May 1974, the Walter E. Heller Foundation, under the leadership of Mrs. Edwin J. DeCosta, pledged a gift of $524,000 to re-create the room and to set up the arch.

No logical and appropriate place for the arch immediately came to mind for the Art Institute. Several locations were considered. One location was on the terrace in front of the Ferguson Wing, where it was proposed by SOM to build a space frame over the arch to shelter it from the elements and so that it could serve as part of a covered entranceway—a gateway—to a rapid transit line then planned that would run under Michigan Avenue. A second location considered was at the northeast corner of Monroe Street and Columbus Drive, apparently to serve as the entryway to the parking garage proposed by the Park District for under the park north of Monroe Street. The third site considered was across Columbus Drive from the museum in Grant Park.

The final suggested location, and the one chosen (see Chronology, p. 23, fig. 36), was on the Art Institute's own block, at the southwest corner of Columbus Drive and Monroe Street. There were several problems involved with this location, however. One concerned the orientation of the arch: no matter which way it was placed, as long as it was freestanding it would always have its unornamented back facing either the museum or the city. In the end, it was decided that the decorated side should face south, toward the museum. This provided the best viewing, but it meant that it served much less well as a visual gateway from the park into the mu-

FIGURE 25. Walter Netsch of Skidmore, Owings and Merrill. Composite photograph showing the elevation of the East Wing and School additions against the Chicago skyline.

FIGURE 26. View from the south of the East Wing addition and of *The Celebration of the 200th Anniversary of the Founding of the Republic* (1976) by Isamu Noguchi (born 1904). The glass wall forms the exterior of the corridor around the reconstructed Trading Room.

seum complex. In order to retain its actual physical function as a gateway, the architects proposed using it as a monumental entrance at the end of a tunnel connecting across Monroe Street to the entrance to the new garage.[58] Unfortunately, the tunnel was never built. The architects also originally proposed that the arch mark one end of a long public promenade through the museum buildings from Columbus Drive to Michigan Avenue. This would have provided a sheltered pathway and would have helped entice the public into the museum, where they could turn from the passage into the various galleries. But this plan proved to be too difficult for security and other reasons.[59] The final result was that today the arch stands free in space without function and turns its back on the city, conditions that trouble many observers.[60]

The salvaged fragments of the Trading Room were used to recreate what the original room looked like in the years immediately after the Stock Exchange building was erected, but before remodelings started in 1908 (see Chronology, pp. 22–23, fig. 35). Originally to be called Louis Sullivan Hall, the room was to serve as an entry area and as a room for large receptions and other events. The architects therefore decided to place the hall at the center of their composition. This decision led to several other major moves. Because Netsch wished to keep the central block low so the pediment of Gunsaulus Hall could be seen over it from Lake Shore Drive and the park (see fig. 25), he decided to lower the level of the hall half a flight below the level of Columbus Drive. On either side, the roof slopes upward symmetrically, one side to the School and the other to the members' lounge and trustees' room, creating what the architects called a "reverse pediment." Another needed change was to shift the entrance from the front of the building, on axis with McKinlock Court and the rest of the buildings, to a side wall at a forty-five-degree angle from the Trading Room. This meant that arriving visitors would come in at a

diagonal to McKinlock Court and the axis of the rest of the building, something that some visitors find disorienting. On the exterior, Netsch wrapped a corridor around the Trading Room and covered the whole with a skin of reflecting mirrored glass which marks the center of the building's east facade (see fig. 26). The architects intended this part of the complex to serve both as a memorial to Louis Sullivan and as gallery space for the display of architectural fragments. The architectural gallery, which would have been housed in the corridor connecting the east entry with the School, never came to be, however.

The re-creation of the Trading Room itself was done under the direction of restoration architect John Vinci and occasioned a round of disputes, often heated, between Vinci and the architects from SOM.[61] These involved both the design of the room and the appropriate manner in which to respond to what was an insufficient budget. In the end, the reconstructed room was very close to the original Trading Room, and the Heller Foundation increased its gift to cover the additional costs.[62] Work on the room went forward slowly, with meticulous attention to detail and with the contributions of a number of highly skilled craftsmen. Although there was a chorus of praise for the appearance of the new room, there was some debate about the philosophical problems of re-creating it in a museum, and some criticism of its location and its lack of clear function.[63]

The landscaping around the new wing was designed by the office of SOM.[64] Although quite different in appearance from the gardens in front of the Ferguson and Morton wings, it incorporated similar elements. The east garden, as it was called, includes a series of terraces at the northeast corner of the site that, responding to the building's forty-five-degree geometries, are trapezoidal in shape. The terraces step down toward the Stock Exchange arch and a small pool. Directly in front of the glass facade of the new building, a large reflecting pool was constructed for which a sculpture was commissioned from Isamu Noguchi (b. 1904). The sculpture (see fig. 26), entitled *The Celebration of the 200th Anniversary of the Founding of the Republic*, was dedicated on November 30, 1976. Mechanical and structural engineers from SOM advised on the plumbing and on the foundation for the pool and sculpture. Finally, another set of steps in front of the School building leads down to a partially sunken court area.[65]

Construction on the new wing was begun in May 1974 and finished in 1977. The new addition was, for the most part, received favorably in the press, and the building won a national honor award from the American Institute of Architects.[66] One complaint, however, was that the new gallery spaces had not been worked out well enough for the specific functions they might house, and a great deal of shuffling around of spaces ensued. It was reported that the second floor of McKinlock Court, for example, was originally intended for textiles, but the large windows would have been unsuitable for the display of light-sensitive fabrics. It was also thought that the very high walls of the space would be ideal for twentieth-century art, but the lack of elevators large enough to bring up oversize canvases made this use problematic. Finally, one half of the space was turned over to art of Africa, Oceania, and the Americas and the other half to twentieth-century painting and sculpture.

A relatively minor, but heavily publicized, problem was the matter of the staircases near the east entry. Because the Stock Exchange Trading Room is located below the level of the Columbus Drive entry, it required a

fairly complicated zone of circulation. The layout was made considerably more complex by the decision to let the sides of the staircases follow the diagonals of the plan, resulting in shapes and spaces that are visually interesting but that are highly disconcerting to some museum visitors. The set of stairs running from the level of the Trading Room up to the lobby, and another stairway down to the lower-level cafeteria, proved to be the most problematic. Here the forty-five-degree angle resulted in stairs that splayed dramatically from top to bottom. This was apparently compounded by the decision, made well after the plans were underway, to reduce costs by shortening the bay module for the entire building.[67] Because the vertical distance between levels remained constant while the horizontal dimensions shrank, the steps ended up being steeper than anticipated. Although such stairs were probably not a real safety hazard, they did tend to disorient museum visitors and, eventually, at the museum's request, they were redesigned by SOM and rebuilt.[68]

When the doors to the new East Wing were finally thrown open, the Art Institute staff and visitors once again breathed a sigh of relief. Another round of building had come to an end. The constant noise of construction was finally stilled and, once again, the controversies surrounding the design decisions would start to recede into the past. But, by the late 1970s, the Art Institute, like other large, successful urban museums, had become much more than a suite of rooms in which to hang Old Master paintings. The museum galleries must now accommodate blockbuster traveling exhibitions, television monitors for video art, and the activities of performance artists. Steeply rising attendance figures have brought with them the need for expanded dining facilities, museum shops, and checkrooms. More ambitious educational and outreach programs require new spaces for lectures and receptions. At the Art Institute, as elsewhere, these changes have been swift and sweeping. They have been deeply disturbing to some who feel that the contact with art has been diminished. On the other hand, the museum has created a vast new constituency and has become more than ever an integral part of the life of the city. All these demands on museums have accelerated the building cycle in institutions across the country. In little more than a decade, the Art Institute trustees had already started to think about phase two, had modified the plans, and had started construction on the next round of remodeling and expansion.

Beaux-Arts Modernism in the Art Institute's Daniel F. and Ada L. Rice Building

STUART KLAWANS, *New York*

WHEN Chicago gave itself over to the World's Columbian Exposition in 1893, the modern city of Dankmar Adler and Louis Sullivan, of Daniel H. Burnham and John Wellborn Root, abruptly came face to face with a fairground of historical fantasies. Almost overnight, a Beaux-Arts stage set arose, bringing plaster versions of the classical architecture of Europe's past into confrontation with the American present. The Shepley, Rutan and Coolidge building for The Art Institute of Chicago (see Phipps, pp. 28–45), constructed as part of the Exposition, was itself an expression of the revival of interest in classical architecture, although it was constructed, not in the fairground, but opposite the modern city on Michigan Avenue.

These events illuminate the curious state of contemporary architecture, which finds the Art Institute today putting up a major new addition entirely in the character of its original, 1893 Allerton Building. More curious still is the fact that the architect, Thomas Beeby, of the Chicago firm of Hammond, Beeby and Babka, sees himself as an exponent of the Chicago School, working in the direct tradition of Louis Sullivan and, especially, Ludwig Mies van der Rohe.[1]

The contradictions between present and past, though, are more apparent than real. The new Daniel F. and Ada L. Rice Building (also called the south building) of the Art Institute (fig. 1) seems a striking anomaly in the landscape of contemporary American museums, as much out of step with other museum expansion projects as it is consistent with the Art Institute's own architecture. But if one gets under the skin of architectural styles, it becomes clear that a classically detailed, Beaux-Arts style building such as this can

FIGURE 1. View from the west across the upper level of the Roger McCormick Memorial Court within the Daniel F. and Ada L. Rice Building, 1988.

indeed be fully modern. A review of current museum architecture also reveals why the unashamed historicism of the Rice Building may be not just a virtue but a necessity, as well. As James N. Wood, director of the Art Institute, claims, the Rice Building—indeed, the Art Institute's whole program of recent changes and renovations—makes a statement about the mission of art museums in America today.

Genesis of the Rice Building

The origins of the Rice Building project lie in a self-study undertaken by the Art Institute in 1980. "We took every department and asked for a status report on where they were . . . and where they hoped to be at the end of the century," Wood says. "We asked for their priorities, to quantify their needs for collections, staff, [and] installation space."[2] The result of these inquiries was a long-range plan that set three goals: increasing the Art Institute's endowment; renovating and restoring the original, 1893 building; and constructing a new building for temporary exhibitions and permanent installations. Once fund-raising was confidently underway, the building projects proceeded simultaneously. Work on the renovation began in August 1984 with the closing of a suite of galleries; construction began in late summer 1985. Work on the new south building began with construction of a new cooling tower in April 1985; work on the building proper began when caissons were laid in December 1985. As Wood explains, the renovation of the galleries of European art (along with the lobby and Grand Staircase; see figs. 2, 3, and back cover) was "as important for its symbolism as its practical accomplishments—we wanted to show our intentions for the Art Institute by restoring its core galleries, which house its best-known collections." The more ambitious project—constructing a new, 128,000-square-foot building at an estimated cost of $23 million—was to complete the reorganization of the Art Institute, fulfilling that symbolism.

FIGURE 2. View of one of the galleries of European art following their renovation in 1987.

FIGURE 3. View from the west of the Grand Staircase and second-floor galleries of European art following their renovation in 1987.

The renovation of the 1893 building, finished in May 1987, drew praise from critics and public alike. Writing in the *New York Times*, John Russell commented that "the redesigned and reinstalled new galleries at the Art Institute of Chicago are by common consent a model of what such things should be." In a companion review, Paul Goldberger wrote that the rooms are "completely in harmony with the building's Beaux-Arts architecture, and they are a clear testament to the fact that there need be no inconsistency between classical architecture and the most up-to-date curatorial attitudes and technological possibilities."[3] "We decided to restore the Beaux-Arts character of the galleries, rather than impose some new and different style on them," James Wood says in retrospect, "and, at that fork in the road, we were right. Perhaps the more important decision came when we asked what style to pick for a major new addition to this institution, and to what degree we should relate it to the original building. Again, the path we chose was one of continuity."

FIGURE 4. View across the Roger McCormick Memorial Court into one of the rooms
within the Field-McCormick Galleries of
American Arts.

But it is one thing to renew a classical container for a collection of European art, and something else to undertake new construction in harmony
with it. Wood identifies the three complementary requirements of the building's program: "functions we wanted, limitations we had to impose, and,
finally, a set of symbolic aspirations." When discussing the functions of the
Rice Building, Wood consistently begins with the one that seems most at
odds with a Beaux-Arts project. "We needed a space for all our special
exhibitions. We wanted the exhibitions to take place in optimum circumstances no matter the material involved, from fragile works on paper to the
most massive stone sculptures." Indeed, at 19,330 square feet, the special-
exhibitions area within the Rice Building, named Regenstein Hall, is one of
the largest in any American art museum, and it is adjoined by 23,910 square
feet of support spaces for the loading dock, storage, carpentry and paint
shops, education, marketing services and art storage.

The role of the Rice Building becomes still more complex when one
considers its other function: to provide gallery space for three of the permanent collections. The Field-McCormick Galleries of American Arts contain
19,160 square feet for a collection of works ranging from the colonial period
to the end of the nineteenth century (fig. 4). The Roger McCormick Memorial Court (see cover and fig. 1), a daylit space for the display of American

sculpture, accounts for another 10,620 square feet. A large portion of the collection of twentieth-century American painting and sculpture has been relocated into 7,835 square feet of gallery space (fig. 5). Finally, the Department of European Decorative Arts and Sculpture has taken over 9,520 square feet, for the display of works from the mid-seventeenth century through the present (fig. 6).

Having established these functions for the new building, the Art Institute then imposed a set of limitations. "The floor space of the building was going to be enormous, but the height had to be low, since by law the building could be no taller than the Art Institute's original, three-story structure." Moreover, says Wood, "The axis has to be north-south, so it would relate logically to the Art Institute's existing main axis, which runs east-west. And we decided the facade had to be understated and reserved. We didn't want it to upstage the original facade on Michigan Avenue, which gives the Art Institute its visual identity and which should remain the main entrance. We asked, rather, that the primary architectural character of the new building be on the inside."

On top of these demands, the Art Institute gave the architects a set of symbolic goals. "One was to provide a timeless and inspiring approach to the temporal, changing exhibitions. We also wanted the building to reinforce and help unify our institutional identity. We wanted them to respect the tradition of this building, yet give us a modern building for a city that is celebrated for its modern architecture. All we really asked for," says Wood, summing up, "was the solution to the central problem of twentieth-century museums: how to make a building that is a statement in itself and for its own time, yet that functions as a container for the art of other people and other times."

The Rice Building from the Architects' Viewpoint

To carry out this project, the Art Institute chose the Chicago architectural firm of Hammond, Beeby and Babka. Thomas Beeby, director of design for the firm, has long-established ties to Chicago. Born in Oak Park, he was educated at Cornell University and received his master's degree in architecture from Yale University. He entered the firm of C.F. Murphy Associates after completing his education in 1965. One of Beeby's first jobs with the firm was on their 1965–67 renovation of the Art Institute's Ryerson and Burnham Libraries. Beeby's identification with the Miesian tradition in Chicago was strengthened through his teaching at the Illinois Institute of Technology from 1973 to 1980. It is tangibly evident in the design details of his buildings from this period, such as the First National Bank of Ripon, Wisconsin, of 1976 and even in the Champaign Public Library of 1977. In 1980, Beeby became director of the School of Architecture at the University of Illinois at Chicago. In 1986, he was named dean of the Yale University School of Architecture, a position he still holds, commuting between New Haven and his office in Chicago. His partner, Bernard Babka, director of technical, production, and office practice for the firm, also shares in the Miesian tradition. Babka was educated at IIT and worked at C.F. Murphy

FIGURE 5. View of the installation of twentieth-century American painting and sculpture on the second floor of the Rice Building.

FIGURE 6. View of the installation of European decorative arts on the lower floor of the Rice Building.

Associates as director of technical services before becoming a principal of Hammond, Beeby and Babka.

The firm's identification with the city was important to the Art Institute, but so was its reputation for a deeply thoughtful, historically based architecture. As Babka comments, "It's part of our philosophy to think of buildings as modern in terms of the technical solutions but not necessarily in terms of architectural solutions." Thomas Beeby adds, "We've attempted to meld the two traditions of modern architecture, particularly as they exist in Chicago. Our notion is that structurally expressive architecture and classical architecture aren't necessarily opposites." The firm has succeeded with this philosophy in previous public projects, most notably the Conrad Sulzer Regional Library, Chicago (1982 Citation of *Progressive Architecture*, National Design Awards Program; 1987 National Honor Award, American Institute of Architects). But the Rice Building is the greatest test by far.

In terms of technical solutions, the challenges began with the problem of maintaining the temperature in the existing building while construction played havoc with the heating and cooling facilities. The Art Institute's cooling tower stood on the construction site and had to be torn down. The design also called for the new building to extend into the space occupied by the boiler plant, but the latter would have been too expensive to replace. "We installed a new cooling tower during the heating season," Babka explains, "so that when the next cooling season came, we could abandon the existing cooling towers and have the new cooling tower on line. We did that in 1985, before any of the real construction started." In the case of the boiler plant, however, there was only one solution: to build over it. The architects managed to accomplish both tasks without violating the rule set by the museum's conservation department that neither heating nor cooling be shut down for more than three hours at a time.

Next, the architects faced a directly related problem, Chicago's severe climate. According to Babka,

The Art Institute had given us criteria for temperature and humidity. And they knew the standards they wanted to set in the South Building were higher than those in the existing buildings. Some of those buildings were put up before there was any real knowledge about vapor barriers. And they found out that if they tried to maintain the humidities they wanted during the cold weather, the outside walls would self-destruct because of the amount of moisture they were putting into them. We also knew that it's very difficult to complete a good vapor barrier in a building where you're trying to maintain temperatures and humidities at those levels.

The solution was to build something akin to a thermos bottle. Just as a thermos has an insulating vacuum between its core and its shell, the Rice Building would use the service areas as a protective layer of insulation between the galleries and the outside wall (figs. 7, 8). "When you put the service areas on the side," says Babka, "you never have to go into a gallery area for maintenance. It's a little more expensive, pushing all that stuff to the outside, but in the long run it makes everything much easier."

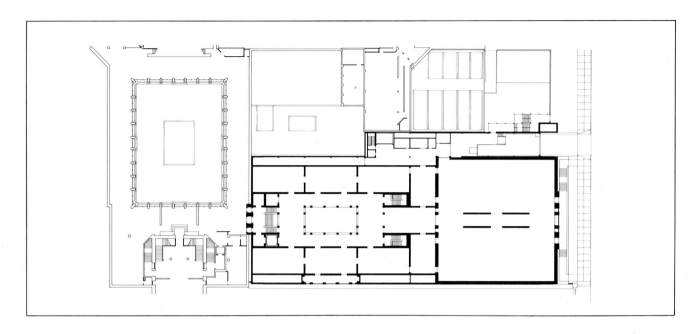

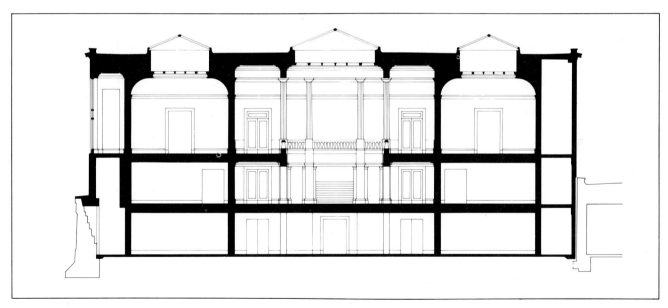

FIGURE 7. Hammond, Beeby and Babka, architects. Plan of the second floor of the Rice Building, showing galleries for twentieth-century American painting and sculpture and Regenstein Hall, 1986.

FIGURE 8. Hammond, Beeby and Babka. Section of the Rice Building, 1986.

The thermos-bottle construction resulted in multiple wall treatments—as many as six or eight different combinations, depending on the kind of space that flanks either side of the wall. The exterior facing of the building is limestone. Behind it comes an airspace, insulation, a concrete-block backup wall, a vapor-barrier coating on the concrete block, and three coats of epoxy finish paint. These materials constitute the outer wall of the service space. The inner wall between the service area and the gallery is constructed of metal-stud drywall, plywood with a vapor barrier of polyethylene film, and, finally, drywall with stretched fabric.

The use of natural light in the galleries posed a related problem. The Art Institute is committed to using natural light, enhanced and controlled as necessary, for the display of paintings and sculpture. The success of the recently renovated Allerton Building galleries has been attributed, in part, to the technically improved, toplit galleries. But the construction of skylights is no easy matter, especially given Chicago's extreme temperatures. The solution, says Babka, came through consultation with lighting designer Claude Engle:

You can take one of two basic approaches. One is to design the system for the winter sun and then figure out how to shade the summer sun when it comes in. The other is to design for the summer sun and let the galleries go darker during the winter. We wanted to keep the light level as high as the conservators would allow, for as long a period of the year as possible without introducing artificial light, so we chose to design around the winter sun. Then we tried a number of shading devices and settled on using adjustable blinds mounted directly below the skylights. The result should be an even light in the galleries throughout the year.

The final technical challenge was to accommodate the multitude of changes required for special exhibitions in Regenstein Hall. In addition to variations

FIGURE 9. View from the south of the Jackson Boulevard facade of the Rice Building.

FIGURE 10. Hammond, Beeby and Babka. Partial elevations of six Art Institute structures, showing comparative treatments of exterior walls, 1986. *Left to right:* Allerton Building, Gunsaulus Hall, Ferguson Building, Morton Wing, East Wing, and Rice Building.

in lighting, temperature and humidity, and security controls, Regenstein Hall will often be sub-divided. The Art Institute will frequently have more than one exhibition in the hall, or will have one on view while another is being prepared. In response, says Babka, "we've developed a ceiling-grid system that will look like a higher-class lay-in ceiling. The grid itself will be used as a return-air system, as well as the lighting track; its lay-in capability will allow the Art Institute staff to push up a panel and make whatever changes the exhibition demands in security and smoke detection. We're also developing a way of attaching temporary partitions to the track system so you won't damage the panels." The ducts and temperature and humidity controls run over the space linearly on fourteen-foot modules, with separate temperature controls so that the hall can easily be divided into zones.

All of these technical innovations make the new south building sound like a modern structure with state-of-the-art facilities. And indeed it is. To the visitor, though, it should not appear to be new. "Ideally," says Beeby, "when you go through the museum, it will be difficult to tell at what point in history the different buildings were constructed. It might even be possible to perceive ours as the initial building, and the others as a large addition to it— if it works correctly." Certainly, with its gray limestone facade (figs. 9, 10), its classical detailing, its skylights and laylights in the top-floor galleries— above all with its two-level, daylit sculpture court with fluted columns (fig. 11)—the south building looks and feels like an old-fashioned, Beaux-Arts museum.

From Beaux-Arts to Modernism

If the criteria of modernism are that a building be structurally expressive and stripped of ornamentation, then, of course, neoclassicism and modernism are at odds. But if one seeks as the definition of modernism a rationalization and abstraction of form, modular construction, and a concern for the way a

FIGURE 11. Partial view of columns surrounding the Roger McCormick Memorial Court on the second floor of the Rice Building.

building expresses its function, then it is clear that the two movements are related, since all of these characteristics were present in neoclassical architecture in the eighteenth century. Furthermore, the Beaux-Arts academic tradition of the nineteenth century added to neoclassicism two of the distinguishing marks of the modern movement: a concern for structural expression and a somewhat abstract method of composing spaces.

John Zukowsky, curator of the Department of Architecture at The Art Institute of Chicago, explains that there has been a decade-long reinterpretation of the Chicago School, revising the reading of architectural history inherited from the Swiss art historian Sigfried Giedion. Because of this reinterpretation, it is no longer possible to set up an easy confrontation between the good early modernists and the bad neoclassicists.

According to Zukowsky, recent research into Chicago architecture of the 1870s, 1880s, and 1890s has shown that Chicago School buildings were simple in appearance because the Boston developers who put them up didn't want to spend their money on ornament. "That's one reason these buildings have a skeletal, stripped-down appearance. The developers in Boston weren't going to see these buildings everyday, so they didn't really care what they looked like." Thus, Chicago School architecture may have looked more modern than the architects themselves would have liked. In much the same way, Daniel Burnham's architecture turned out to be less classical than the ideal he projected in the White City of the 1893 Columbian Exposition and in his 1909 *Plan of Chicago*. Zukowsky comments:

The Flatiron Building was Burnham's *real* world. The White City was his vision of what a city should be. But the reality was that he had to put up big office buildings in order to make money, to keep his firm going. People talk about the Burnham Plan for Chicago in terms of the unifying cornice line. But that was just the dream. He had no intention of building everything just like that. Look out on Michigan Avenue at the buildings Burnham actually put up—Orchestra Hall, the Peoples Gas Building, the Santa Fe Building. Each has a different cornice line. That was the reality. The Plan was just a proposal, a diagram of his ideas.

What this view of history shows is the rich mixture of modernism and neoclassicism that existed in Chicago in 1893. It is one of the tricks of history that this mixture should be visible in the Art Institute itself. Shepley, Rutan and Coolidge converted the 1893 building into a home for the Art Institute from 1894 through 1910; but, even then, the building, as originally planned, remained incomplete. Today, over the Grand Staircase, some of the steel skeleton remains exposed, as if to demonstrate that this building began as a glorious vision and became a piecemeal reality. Here, the Art Institute is structurally expressive by default.

The Rice Building from the Visitor's Viewpoint

Thomas Beeby has acknowledged that his firm is really completing a work of Chicago architecture: "Because the Art Institute was built in phases, it never had any overall plan—it was never completed in a coherent way. It's only now, I think, with the renovation project and the new building, that it will be coherent." Just as Wood stresses historical continuity as the justification for the south building's style, so does Beeby return again and again to the theme of coherence, not so much as it is expressed externally in the building's appearance, but more in terms of the coherence of the visitor's experience.

"There has been a kind of loss of memory about what classical architecture is supposed to do." In Beeby's view, the hallmark of the Beaux-Arts system—the axial structure of a building—allows you "to see where you're going and where you've been, so you always have a sense of the whole building." In designing the Rice Building, Beeby took the existing axial structure of the Art Institute as his starting point.

Our idea is to reinforce the initial design concept, to play on it, elaborate it. The existing building has a linear axis that runs west to east, from Michigan Avenue to Columbus Drive. That axis has a recurring series of light-wells or skylights or courtyards, which punctuate your passage. The new south building runs on the cross-axis and introduces a top-lit courtyard, which is a play on that theme.

The two-level sculpture court is the chief feature of the new structure that enables a visitor to orient himself. It is the key to the building's character. "As you walk through [the south building]," Beeby says, "you'll have a series of sub-axial developments because of the way the doors relate across the courtyard. In a typically classical way, you'll get not just the relationship from room to room but of the spaces across the court." In addition, there is a series of openings that will let the visitor look out of the south building on to the rest of the Art Institute and to the city itself:

For example, at the center of the new courtyard space on the second floor, the axes of the doors run out into a loggia space, which is along the side of the building adjacent to the railroad tracks. But you're elevated above the tracks, and you have a fantastic view of the city. As you pass through that gallery, there will be doors that open onto this porchlike piece, and you'll be able to look out onto the skyline, over the rest of the Art Institute. Another example: There's a glass link between the old building and the Morton Wing. That lines up more or less with the loggia piece, which means you'll be able to see people walking across to the Morton Wing. You'll have a sense of continuity not only within the south building but within the Art Institute as a whole.

As a further play on this structure, the Art Institute will be able to put major works of art at the axial endpoints. "At the end of every axis, you will have either a primary work from the collection, or a view to the outside, or a view across into another space. This gives the building the sense of repose, yet expansion, that better classical buildings have."

"Repose, yet expansion": Beeby's phrase implies that the visitor's experience of the Rice Building will be active. Ideally, an axial structure, in addition to allowing the visitor to comprehend the building as a whole, also lays out a dramatic progression of spaces, the *promenade architecturelle* as the Beaux-Arts architects knew it. Beeby used just this progression to help integrate the special exhibitions into the Art Institute as a whole.

We made a conscious decision to put the special exhibitions hall at the end of permanent collection space. Because of the nature of special exhibitions, you have to have flexible space, with essentially no architectural character. That's because

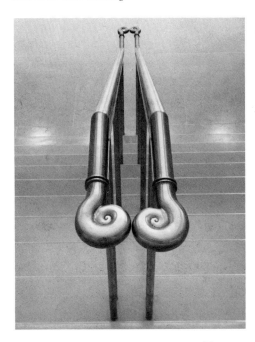

FIGURE 12. View of stainless-steel handrails in the Rice Building.

special exhibitions are like theater, and every show is different. The character of the space has to be established with the installation of each show. But the use of the permanent collection as a frontispiece establishes the Beaux-Arts character on the way to the special exhibitions. It creates a ceremonial, processional, celebratory aspect to going to see a temporary event.

"The architectural spaces you move through as you go toward something can make statements," James Wood adds. "They can prepare you for something elevated, something special—or they can make it a totally mundane, unsymbolic approach. We are trying to create a series of spaces that prepare the visitor for an aesthetic event."

Once again, the issue of symbolism arises—not merely the symbolism of the south building for the Art Institute's peculiar history, but also the symbolism of the art museum itself. To return to a remark of Wood's cited above, the south building is meant to solve "the central problem of twentieth-century museums." Wood makes the statement half-jokingly; but he also believes the Art Institute is setting an example. "Until relatively recently, there was considerable consensus as to the purpose of art museums: what they were supposed to do, why they were doing it, who the audience was. That consensus has disintegrated, and we are faced today with the problem of finding our way through a confusion of identities."

Masterpiece Collections and Modern Additions

While the Rice Building is meant to be a clear statement of the Art Institute's identity, a look at some other notable new museum buildings of the past decade reveals the "confusion of identities" Wood speaks of. There is no better place to begin the tour than with the grandest of American museums, The Metropolitan Museum of Art in New York. In 1970, the Metropolitan decided on a master plan for growth and hired Kevin Roche/John Dinkeloo & Associates to design all the new buildings. To date, five new wings have been built; a sixth and final one is scheduled for completion in the fall of 1990.[4] Although these six additions have all been designed by Kevin Roche and share stylistic traits—notably, the use of insulated, tempered glass and aluminum framing—they make no attempt to match the original design of the Metropolitan (figs. 13, 14). Indeed, the museum has paid no attention to architectural consistency. "From above," writes critic Douglas Davis, the Metropolitan "is an impure labyrinth of wings-upon-wings-upon-wings, none reluctant to defy the architectural 'style' of the other, whether it be Gothic Revival, Italian Renaissance, or the Temple of Dendur. Down near the left of center lurks the tiny 'original' gallery, designed by a forgotten man named Calvert Vaux in 1881."[5]

In the case of the Metropolitan, this indifference to stylistic unity may well be the prerogative of greatness. What is remarkable, however, is the prevalence of this attitude. Perhaps the most influential museum addition in America has been I. M. Pei's 1978 East Building for the National Gallery of Art in Washington, D.C., a structure that pays virtually no attention to the neoclassicism of John Russell Pope's 1941 structure. Indeed, the East Wing has set an example that extends well beyond the art world. Andrea Op-

FIGURE 13. View from the north of the Fifth Avenue facade of The Metropolitan Museum of Art, New York, designed by McKim, Mead and White, 1902. Photo: Brian Rose, The Metropolitan Museum of Art.

94

penheimer Dean, executive editor of *Architecture*, the official magazine of the American Institute of Architects, has commented that

The East Building, with its knife-like edges, minimal, marble facades, and huge skylit atrium ringed with flexible, enclosed perimeter galleries, may well be the nation's last great modern monument. The major elements of its interior configuration have been mimicked in institutional architecture across the land. Look, for instance, at the design of mixed use commercial buildings, corporate buildings, or spec office buildings, with their spacious, often top-lit lobbies, lined with pricey materials. Many, like the East Building, have overhead bridges and balconies, escalators and ramps, and generally all of this leads to cramped elevator banks and office floors with eight-foot ceilings. The East Building's model of grand spaces for public gatherings and approach ringed with more ordinary ones for the display of art was followed by Cesar Pelli, FAIA, in his 1983 addition to the Museum of Modern Art, and [Richard] Meier credits a direct influence of the East Building on the High [Museum in Atlanta], whose focus is a four-story, top-lit drum.[6]

Beeby, too, is well aware of the East Building's precedent, though he is quick to point out a less-than-obvious similarity between Pei's building and Pope's original:

When you look at the control of detail in John Russell Pope's building, you can see it was all resolved on a drawing board. Whereas, in a *real* classical building, a lot was left to the craftsmen. There was a convention in the way you put things together, but because of the way it was resolved in the field there was a messiness in the details that gave it a kind of vitality. You have a sense in the Pope building that everything is totally under control. It has the same character as the East Wing, which has the same kind of compulsive design control. The entire object, right down to the last screw, is under the control of the designer, not the craftsman. So that, although the styles of the two wings of the National Gallery are superficially different, if you get into the sensibility behind them, they're actually quite similar.

Beeby's insight raises the possibility addressed in his own south building: that of designing something that looks and feels old but is modern in its essence. Clearly, Pei's design provided a solution for present architectural needs, but it evaded the challenge of providing a link with the past.

Thus, the Roche addition to the Metropolitan and the National Gallery's East Wing demonstrate the same strategy for dealing with history: avoidance. In its 1986 Robert O. Anderson Building, the Los Angeles County Museum of Art demonstrated another strategy: obliteration. LACMA faced the challenge of expanding a 1960s structure, designed by William Pereira, that was generally disliked. Hardy Holzman Pfeiffer Associates solved the problem with an addition that "squashed the three original buildings," according to one critic, "obscuring everything behind it."[7] Likewise, the proposed addition to the Whitney Museum in New York, designed by Michael Graves, has raised similar objections, specifically, that it will not so much add to Marcel Breuer's original building as absorb it.

A third strategy, which expresses the eclecticism and historicism of recent fashion, is to make the new museum building look modern, but to incorporate a few elements of the design of the old one. There have been successful additions done with this method, such as Hardy Holzman Pfeiffer's 1985

FIGURE 14. View from the north of the Robert Lehman Wing of The Metropolitan Museum of Art, designed by Kevin Roche/John Dinkeloo & Associates, 1975. Photo: Brian Rose, The Metropolitan Museum of Art.

West Wing for the Virginia Museum of Fine Arts.[8] The Brooklyn Museum, heir to a superb Beaux-Arts building by McKim, Mead and White, is following a similar strategy with its proposed expansion (fig. 15). Designed by Arata Isozaki in association with James Stewart Polshek & Partners, the proposal "is a mixture of abstract geometric forms and neo-classical elements that are to be recreated from the original 1893 design. The proposal includes a 150-foot-high skylighted obelisk, to be an evocative architectural centerpiece alluding to the museum's Egyptian collection."[9]

This third strategy makes use of the symbolic methods introduced by Robert Venturi in his *Complexity and Contradiction in Architecture*, which has, since its publication in 1966, gone the whole route from heresy to dogma.[10] Postmodernism has freed architects to be something more than structurally expressive; but it has also brought them back in some ways to problems last faced a century ago. Vincent Scully has remarked that the eclectic method of the mid-nineteenth century was "purely one of optical titillation. . . . This was true even of Victorian Gothic design, however desperately iconological, 'realistic,' and structural it tried to be." Ransacking history in search of new combinations, the nineteenth century "re-enacted the entire course of western architecture and finally managed to work its way back to a kind of pseudo-baroque design, drained of emotional focus and of meanings other than theatrical ones."[11] That contemporary architecture runs a similar risk of recapitulating this process with modernism thrown in as just another catalogue style by now has become obvious.

In this context, the approach adopted by Beeby at the Art Institute—of postmodern historicism pursued with modernist rigor—begins to seem almost polemical. Wood cautions that the south building should not be seen as slavishly imitative. "It's interpretative classicizing. There's hardly a line in this building that was taken one-for-one from any precedent. What you get, rather, is Karl Friedrich Schinkel, seen through the Beaux-Arts, seen through Tom Beeby." For all that, it is impossible to see the south building without understanding that it is making a statement. What, finally, is its message?

Classicism as Populism

When the Art Institute restored the Beaux-Arts character of its galleries of European art, its reasoning was as much practical as symbolic. The museum realized that the original floor plan worked for the public. As Beeby has noted, classical design allows the visitor to understand the building as a whole. It also offers a certain freedom of choice: the floor plan lets visitors choose what they want to see and proceed at their own pace. Classicism does impose a sense of drama on the visitor, and in that sense might be called coercive; but it also implies that the visitor is an actor in the space, rather than, say, a consumer. Wood summarizes the arguments in favor of classical design by noting: "The building is there for you to use, rather than for you to try to climb your way through."

If classicism, then, lends a certain dignity to the institution, it also allows

FIGURE 15. Arata Isozaki and James Stewart Polshek & Partners, architects. Aerial view of model showing The Brooklyn Museum and proposed addition, 1986. Photo: The Brooklyn Museum.

the people who use the museum to feel a dignity of their own. Again, James Wood:

Every group in our city, every ethnic group and every social class, wants to partake in the civic advantages of the community. We therefore have to look for a way to be welcoming without abandoning our sense of historical prestige. We've learned that people from all backgrounds and social levels want to participate in great institutions. They don't want to have institutions scaled down to a common denominator; they don't want to remove the monumental facade and the grand staircase. Maybe it's less intimidating for people to come in right off the street, possibly through the back door. It's certainly easier—but in a sense, it's also condescending.

The neoclassicism of the Rice Building, then, is in no way reactionary. Rather, it looks back to a time just before modernism happened, when populist dreams and practical realities conspired for a moment, creating both a White City and great precursors of the modern movement. In a sense, the south building will make good on the promise of that moment. Using the techniques of modernism, it will realize a Beaux-Arts vision of 1893.

Is this neoclassical solution applicable to museums and civic institutions in general? Possibly not. The Rice Building indeed makes a statement about the civic possibilities of art museums today; but its strongest message has to do with the identity of the Art Institute itself. Asked about his ultimate goal for

FIGURE 16. View from the east of the loggia on the second floor of the Rice Building.

the south building, Beeby replies that he has tried to deal with the memories the Art Institute evokes.

The great thing about museums is that everyone has memories of visiting them, starting from childhood and going all through your life. Our attempt was to be true to our memories, so that we wouldn't disrupt the experience, the sense one has from having used the building, of what the building should be. We were trying not to rupture the memory of everyone who uses that museum. People will see the south building as a logical extension of their memories of what the museum is all about. I think that's actually what cultural continuity is about. It's something architects should strive for.

NOTES

Phipps, The 1893 Building, pp. 28–45.

1. The Exposition directors' decision to place most of the buildings in Jackson Park may have spurred A. Montgomery Ward, a prosperous Chicago merchant and a governing member of the Art Institute, in his legal actions concerning the appearance of Lake Park. On October 16, 1890, Ward filed suit against the city, demanding that the lakefront be cleared of the refuse, wooden shanties (some of which housed brothels and taverns) and other haphazardly constructed buildings on the public ground that was to remain "forever open, clear and free" of buildings or other obstructions, as stated in the original 1836 Canal Commissioner's plat. Lois Wille discussed the history of the development of the lakefront in *Forever Open, Clear and Free: The Historic Struggle for Chicago's Lakefront* (Chicago, 1972).

2. *Chicago Tribune*, October 12, 1890.

3. The 1885–87 Art Institute building was clad in Connecticut brownstone and Denver red sandstone, and ornamented with bas-reliefs.

4. Hutchinson was president of the Commerical Club in 1889. Thomas J. Schlereth discussed the participation of the Art Institute trustees in the Commercial Club's civic-improvement projects in "Big Money and High Culture: The Commercial Club of Chicago and Charles L. Hutchinson," *The Great Lakes Review: A Journal of Midwestern Culture* 3, 1 (summer 1976), pp. 15–27. The Commercial Club of Chicago was a somewhat exclusive organization with a limited membership. For a list of other civic concerns addressed by this organization, see John J. Glessner, *The Commercial Club of Chicago, Its Beginnings and Something of Its Work* (Chicago, 1910), p. 14.

5. Glessner (note 4), p. 148.

6. Ibid.

7. Governing members were elected by the Art Institute trustees. Upon election, they paid $100 and subsequent annual dues of $10. Only governing members could be elected to or vote for the Board of Trustees.

8. See Solon S. Beman, *Scrapbook of Architectural Designs, Plans and Details, mostly executed by Solon S. Beman, 1853–1914*, Chicago Historical Society, library, unpag. The newspaper clipping on which Beman's drawing appears is undated, but must have been published before October 1890. A similar illustration entitled "Proposed Improvements on the Lake Front" by Telford Burnham and James Gookins (a developer and an architect) appeared in the *Daily Inter-Ocean* on November 15, 1890. This scheme, never mentioned by the Art Institute trustees, featured a Palace of Fine Arts in a Baroque revival style. A copy of this illustration can be found in Linda S. Phipps, "The Art Institute of

Chicago 1890–97: Patrons and Architects" (M.A. thesis, University of Wisconsin-Madison, 1986).

9. In a letter from A. W. Sawyer to D. H. Burnham dated September 19, 1890, Sawyer stated that Charles Hutchinson wished to see some drawings by Beman for "some buildings on the Lakefront." "Burnham, D. H., Letters, Business and Personal," Daniel H. Burnham Papers (microfilm, 1890–91, vols. 1–2), Ryerson and Burnham Libraries, The Art Institute of Chicago.

10. Harriet Monroe, *John Wellborn Root: A Study of His Life and Work* (New York, 1896; rpt. Park Forest, Ill., 1966). See specifically pp. 234, 247, 252–54.

11. Since R. C. MacLean, editor of the *Inland Architect*, was a close friend of Root's, this information was most likely accurate. See "Synopsis of Building News," *The Inland Architect and News Record* 13 (Apr. 1889), p. 60.

12. See American Institute of Architects Board of Directors, *Proceedings of the Twenty-fourth Annual Convention of the American Institute of Architects*, John W. Root, ed. (Chicago, 1891), p. 111.

13. Monroe (note 10), pp. 252–54.

14. Dora Louise Root to Charles L. Hutchinson, March 4, 1891. Charles Lawrence Hutchinson Papers, The Newberry Library, Chicago.

15. D. H. Burnham to Francis M. Whitehouse, May 15, 1891, in "Burnham, D. H., Letters, Business and Personal" (note 9).

16. Although Burnham's official reason for giving the Palace of Fine Arts to Atwood was that Whitehouse was too ill to complete the job, he later told his biographer Charles Moore that he had taken the job away from the firm because "they did not seem to grasp the work aright. . . ." Typed manuscript of interview with Charles Moore, "Scrapbooks," Daniel H. Burnham Papers, vol. 3, p. 9, Ryerson and Burnham Libraries, The Art Institute of Chicago.

17. From *The Reminiscences of Augustus Saint-Gaudens*, cited in Donald Hoffmann, *The Architecture of John Wellborn Root* (Baltimore and London, 1973), p. 220. Atwood's building, originally executed in staff (a mixture of plaster of paris, hemp fibers, and portland cement—an inexpensive, impermanent material) over a brick and iron core, was made permanent in 1929 by Burnham's successor firm, Graham, Anderson, Probst and White. After the Fair, the building served as the first home of what later became the Field Museum of Natural History and, later still, it became the Museum of Science and Industry.

18. D. H. Burnham to C. L. Hutchinson, September 8, 1891. Burnham included the text of McKim's telegram in his letter, appealing to the authority of the Eastern architectural establishment. "Burnham, D. H., Letters, Business and Personal" (note 9). See also *Harper's Weekly: A Journal of Civilization* 35, 1811 (Sept. 5, 1891), pp. 681–82.

19. The Illinois Inter-State Industrial Exposition Company was organized in 1873 by hotel owner and merchant Potter Palmer and others as part of a booster campaign to get Chicago back on its feet after the 1871 Fire. Though intended as a one-time effort, the exposition became a yearly event, featuring art exhibits and concerts by the Theodore Thomas Orchestra (which became the Chicago Symphony). Because it provided an early example of local businessmen's dual concerns for business and cultural growth in the city, and because of its cultural and civic nature, as well as its temporary status, the Inter-State Industrial Exposition building was allowed to remain in Lake Park indefinitely. The building may have been a precedent for the ordinance of 1891 granting ownership of the proposed Art Institute building to the city but allowing the museum tenancy for as long as it desired. The building was still standing in 1892, when it was demolished to make way for the new Art Institute structure.

20. Concessions made by the Art Institute under the terms of the 1891 ordinance included allowing the mayor and the city comptroller to become ex officio members of the Board of Trustees, agreeing to furnish the city with an annual financial statement of the Art Institute's operations, and agreeing to free admission to the museum for Chicago public school teachers. In addition, certain days were to be designated as "free" days for the public. The Art Institute of Chicago, *Annual Report of the Trustees for the Year Ending June 2, 1891* (Chicago, 1891), pp. 17–19.

21. For an excellent study of the philanthropic activities of Chicago businessmen, see Helen Lefkowitz Horowitz, *Culture and the City: Cultural Philanthropy in Chicago from the 1880s to 1917* (Lexington, Ky., 1976).

22. Clipping from the *Chicago Tribune*, June 19, 1891, in *Chicago Art Institute Scrapbooks* (vol. 5, 1891). See also the minutes of the December 12, 1891, meeting, *Chicago Academy of Fine Arts/Records, 1879–91*, p. 224. Ryerson and Burnham Libraries, The Art Institute of Chicago.

23. Daniel H. Burnham, "Charles Bowler Atwood," *The Inland Architect and News Record* 26, 6 (Jan. 1896), pp. 56–57. Burnham's comments were echoed by Rossiter Johnson in *History of the World's Columbian Exposition Held in Chicago in 1893* (Chicago, 1897), vol. 1, pp. 172–73. Johnson attributed over seventy buildings to Atwood. These comments reveal more about Burnham's attitude toward Atwood than about his chief designer's productivity. The numerous buildings designed and erected by Burnham's Department of Construction were apparently attributed by Burnham to Atwood either out of respect for the designer after his death in 1895 or as a point of protocol. It is unlikely that Atwood alone would have been able to design so many buildings in such a short time. A few drawings of the buildings attributed to Atwood bear the names of other draftsmen, suggesting that several designs may be attributed to members of the large team of draftsmen that Atwood supervised.

24. There are nine letters from H. H. Richardson to George Shepley, dating from December 1885 to March 1886, that provide a clear picture of the degree to which Richardson relied on the younger man to help him run his office during the last few months of his life. Richardson died on April 27, 1886. Shepley Bulfinch Richardson and Abbott, architects, Henry Hobson Richardson Manuscript Collection, Houghton Library, Harvard University, Cambridge, Mass. (on deposit).

25. The author is grateful to Robert Roche, archivist at Shepley Bulfinch Richardson and Abbott, for this information. According to Mr. Roche, Shepley, Rutan and Coolidge also designed a residence for Albert A. Sprague during the 1890s on North State Street. When Hutchinson and Ryerson left in late December 1891 for Egypt, Sprague joined the building committee to vote on some of the important later design decisions.

26. Even though only two firms had officially been invited, Beman, as stated earlier, proposed a plan that was published in the *Chicago Evening Mail*. George L. Healy (1856–?) and Louis J. Millet (1855–1923) were the principal members of a local interior design firm that did much work for Adler and Sullivan. They also decorated the interior of Fullerton Memorial Hall (Shepley, Rutan and Coolidge, 1898) for the Art Institute; after the dissolution of the partnership in 1899, Millet designed the skylight for the Ryerson Library in 1901. Millet also designed the Art Institute's first corporate seal in 1891. David Hanks discussed Millet's work for the Art Institute in "Louis J. Millet and the Art Institute of Chicago," *The Art Institute of Chicago Bulletin* 67 (Mar.–Apr. 1973), pp. 13–19. Perhaps Healy and Millet submitted interior designs to complement some of the early projects for the 1892-93 Art Institute building, although the trustees never specified the exact nature of their contribution.

27. Minutes of the October 17, 1891, meeting, Chicago Academy of Fine Arts/Records, *1879–91*, pp. 217–18. Ryerson and Burnham Libraries, The Art Institute of Chicago.

28. See Chicago Architectural Sketch Club, *Catalogue, Seventh Annual Exhibition, Chicago Architectural Sketch Club, The Art Institute, Chicago, May 1894* (Chicago, 1894). Entry number twenty-one was a "Competitive Design for the Chicago Art Institute" in pen and ink by Atwood, but it was not among those illustrated. In the same catalogue, Chicago sculptor Johannes Gelert, a close friend of Root's, published his "Design for Pediment of Art Institute" (no number). If Gelert designed this pediment to accompany Atwood's competitive design, it is logical to deduce that Atwood's project had a large central pediment. According to the *Inland Architect* 22, 5 (Dec. 1893), p. 47, Philip Martiny designed the pedimental sculpture that was never executed for the Shepley, Rutan and Coolidge building.

29. Atwood died on December 19, 1895. See *Catalogue of the Tenth Annual Exhibition of Works of Architecture and the Allied Fine Arts Held Under the Auspices of the Chicago*

Architectural Club at the Art Institute of Chicago, March 23–April 11, 1897 (Chicago, 1897). Entries fourteen through twenty-five were by Atwood; number twenty-six was a portrait of the late architect; and number nineteen, "First Sketch for the Art Institute of Chicago," may have been a sketch preliminary to the competition.

30. These photographs, presumably taken by someone in the firm of Shepley, Rutan and Coolidge, perhaps for archival purposes (each one has been numbered in ink in the upper right corner and mounted on tagboard), are undated and unsigned. The tattered state of the northern elevation drawing evident from the photograph indicates that the photographs were made of the drawing after they had been returned to the firm. According to Robert Roche, a number of the firm's drawings and other records from the Boston office were discarded during the 1930s. The records of the Chicago office of Shepley, Rutan and Coolidge passed into the possession of Charles Hodgdon after Coolidge's death. Efforts to trace these have proved unsuccessful.

31. The drawings are part of the collection of architectural drawings in the Burnham Library of Architecture in the Art Institute. These early working drawings can be dated by the Chicago address of the firm, at 230 LaSalle Street, in the upper left corner of drawing number seven. This is the address of the Gaff Building, the location of the first Chicago offices of Shepley, Rutan and Coolidge. The opening of these offices was noted in *The Inland Architect and News Record* 18, 6 (Jan. 1892), p. 79.

32. The engraving entitled "The Art Institute of Chicago" (fig. 13) represents the building as actually constructed (except for the order of the artists' names on the entablature). However, the same engraving was published in *The Inland Architect and News Record* 19, 1 (Feb. 1892), n. p., with the caption "Proposed Building for The Art Institute of Chicago," suggesting the tentative quality of the design. The second engraving of the set (fig. 12), also entitled "Proposed Building for The Art Institute of Chicago," represents a building closer to the competition design.

33. Please note that the small numbers in the upper right corners of these photographs do not appear on the originals. These numbers (twenty-three, twenty-five, twenty-six) were apparently inscribed in the photographs by someone at the firm. The fact that they do not form a complete sequence suggests that there were other photographs belonging to this set that have not survived.

34. The production of carefully rendered ink-and-wash presentation drawings such as those in the photographs was so labor-intensive that it would have been unlikely for Shepley, Rutan and Coolidge to have reproduced more than one copy of each. The fact that only photographs, not drawings, remain in the firm's Boston archives, combined with the absence of all other records from the Chicago office, suggests that the only set of drawings remained in Chicago.

35. *The Inland Architect and News Record* 22, 5 (Dec. 1893), p. 47. The comparison between the new Art Institute building and the hemicycle of the Ecole des Beaux-Arts, Paris, decorated by Paul Delaroche's fresco cycle (depicting the chronological evolution of the arts as represented by painters, sculptors, and architects) is particularly interesting in the context of the chronologically ordered inscriptions running around the architrave on the exterior, and of the fresco program represented in the 1894 designs for the domed staircase addition. It is likely that Hutchinson or French would have known of the hemicycle and its significance, particularly since parts of the painting had been reproduced in bas-reliefs on the facade of the Pennsylvania Academy of the Fine Arts in Philadelphia.

36. In 1910, the room formerly designated as the secretary's office was turned into a coat closet, termed " . . . a convenience much needed" in the *32nd Annual Report of the Trustees of The Art Institute of Chicago*, 1911, p. 14.

37. Hutchinson to William Rainey Harper, March 21, 1891. University of Chicago, President's Papers, 1889–1925, Joseph Regenstein Library, University of Chicago.

38. Minutes of the January 7, 1892, meeting of the Board of Trustees of The Art Institute of Chicago, in Meeting Minutes 1891–present, the Office of the Secretary, the Art Institute. *The Inland Architect and News Record* 18, 6 (Jan. 1892), p. 79, reported the opening of the firm's Chicago office in the Gaff Building. It added that Shepley, Rutan and Coolidge "have decided to abandon all offices in other cities." The Chicago office was to be run by Coolidge.

39. The trustees would have been amused by the subtle joke found in the frieze: in place of the names of great artists were the names of officers and trustees of the Art Institute: "Carpenter," "Dole," "Hutchinson," "Gage," and "French." The architects' sense of humor suggests the relaxed atmosphere that must have characterized their interactions with the Art Institute board.

40. The Art Institute possessed plaster casts of fragments of the Panathenaic procession at the time.

41. Drawing number six gives only the Boston address; number seven includes the Chicago address below the Boston one, although it is in a different hand and clearly added later. Undoubtedly, the drawings were prepared in Boston and sent to Chicago. The office in the Gaff Building was not opened until January 1892 (see note 31) and the Ames Building in Boston, also designed by the firm, was not completed until early 1892.

42. Chicago Public Library Board of Directors, Committee on Building and Grounds, Meeting Minutes (Aug. 1891–Dec. 1896), September 5 and 25, 1891. The Chicago Public Library.

43. Leon Battista Alberti's S. Francesco in Rimini (1450) and Henri Labrouste's Bibliothèque Ste.-Geneviève in Paris (1848) are well-known examples.

44. The absence of a strict chronological order in the running inscriptions of the early drawings and engravings of the Art Institute project by Shepley, Rutan and Coolidge was undoubtedly due to the architects' representation of a general idea. Whether the idea of the inscriptions originated with the architects or the trustees is unknown. Both would have been aware of several recent precedents to this idea, most notably on the facade of the Boston Public Library. The notion of a chronological order for the names of the artists was not novel, but the trustees would not have failed to specify their preference in this regard, since it generally reflected the order of their collections.

45. Chicago Public Library Board of Directors (note 42), September 25, 1891.

46. Chicago Public Library Board of Directors (note 42), April 4, May 14 and 26, 1892; February 23, 1893.

47. Jane Clarke, Associate Director of Museum Education, has compiled a chronological list of additions by Shepley, Rutan and Coolidge and their successors, Coolidge and Hodgdon, to the Art Institute, published in John Zukowsky, "The Art Institute of Chicago: Constructions, Concepts, and Queries," *Threshold* 3 (autumn 1985), pp. 60–74; esp. pp. 71–74. This chronology has been updated for this issue of *Museum Studies*: see pp. 7–27.

48. See Zukowsky (note 47).

49. John Zukowsky, Curator of Architecture at the Art Institute, has suggested that the elegant proportions of the saucer dome resemble those of Atwood's Palace of Fine Arts. While it is impossible to ascertain whether this replacement of the strange, "Islamic" proportions of the dome in the competion drawing can be attributed to the increased sophistication of the trustees or to the architects' greater familiarity with academic classicism, several such domes could be found on the buildings at the Exposition. The ready example of Atwood's building, which was still standing in 1894, could easily have influenced the Art Institute trustees. The fact that a winged statue of Victory surmounted the dome in early drawings of Atwood's Palace of Fine Arts, recalling that of the Art Institute competition drawings, further supports this idea.

50. Robert C. Spencer, Jr., was educated at M.I.T., winning the Rotch Traveling Scholarship to Europe in 1891 for his superb draftsmanship. He came to Chicago from the Shepley, Rutan and Coolidge office in Boston. Setting up an independent practice shortly afterwards, he later became associated with the Prairie School. Spencer's drawing was published in J. Seymour Currey, *Chicago: Its History and Its Builders, a Century of Marvelous Growth* (Chicago, 1912), vol. 2, pl. between pp. 266–67. The illustration bore the confident caption: "Dome and Grand stairway of Art Institute, Completed in 1912."

51. See The Art Institute of Chicago, *Preliminary Catalogue to the Elbridge G. Hall Collection of Casts* (Chicago, 1891).

52. See William M. R. French, Notes: Journey to Europe with Mr. and Mrs. Charles L. Hutchinson starting from New York, Saturday, March 9, 1889, Ryerson and Burnham Libraries, Art Institute. The Nike of Samothrace, excavated during the 1870s, had been placed on the Daru Staircase (*Escalier Daru*) in the Musée du Louvre in 1886, shortly after its rostral platform had been uncovered. In this new location, with its shoulders and wings restored, the figure became extremely popular.

53. Hutchinson was certainly instrumental in commissioning the firm to design the Corn Exchange National Bank of Chicago (1908), of which he was president.

54. Shepley, Rutan and Coolidge and their Chicago successors, Coolidge and Hodgdon, designed twenty-three structures for the University of Chicago, including Hutchinson Commons (1903, for Charles Hutchinson), Bartlett Gymnasium (1904, for Art Institute trustee Adolphus C. Bartlett), the Law School (1904), Ryerson Physical Laboratory Annex (1913, for Martin A. Ryerson), and Hicks-McElwee Orthopedic Hospital (1931). Jean F. Block, in *The Uses of Gothic: Planning and Building the Campus of the University of Chicago 1892–1932* (Chicago, 1983), provided a complete building list; see pp. 224–27.

55. Charles Hodgdon to Edwin DeWitt Burton, November 22, 1923. University of Chicago, President's Papers, 1889–1925, Joseph Regenstein Library, University of Chicago.

56. The Chicago Public Library has already been mentioned. Later, the Field Museum of Natural History (1912–15) and the Shedd Aquarium (1923–25) were constructed. During the late 1920s, the renovation and adaptation of the decaying Palace of Fine Arts for the Museum of Science and Industry received wide-spread public support that suggests a general type established in the public mind for museum buildings by the early example of the Allerton Building.

Clarke, The Art Institute's Lions, pp. 47–55.

1. The lions were cast by the American Bronze Founding Company, Chicago, operated by Jules Berchem. Berchem's signature appears with Kemeys's wolf-head symbol on the base of each lion.

2. The Art Institute of Chicago, *Annual Report of the Trustees for the Year Ending June 2, 1891* (Chicago, 1891), pp. 8, 14–21.

3. See the article by Linda Phipps in this issue, pp. 28–45, for a discussion of the Art Institute's 1893 building by the firm of Shepley, Rutan and Coolidge. Two other great temporary halls, built at a cost of $27,000 and each one

holding 3,000 people, had also been erected to serve the Congresses. These halls were demolished immediately after the fair closed on October 31, 1893.

4. *Harper's Weekly: A Journal of Civilization* 35, 1811 (Sept. 1891), p. 681.

5. Ann Van Zanten, "The Marshall Field Annex and the New Urban Order of Daniel Burnham's Chicago," *Chicago History* 11, 3 (1982), p. 130.

6. Daniel H. Burnham, *Report of the Director of Works*, vol. 4, p. 40.

7. Ibid., pp. 56, 57.

8. Rossiter Johnson, ed., *History of the World's Columbian Exhibition Held in Chicago in 1893* (New York, 1897), vol. 1, p. 148.

9. Richard Guy Wilson, *McKim, Mead, and White* (New York, 1983), p. 30.

10. *Report of the Board of General Managers of the Exhibit of the State of New York at the World's Columbian Exposition* (New York, 1894), pp. 95–96.

11. Ibid.

12. Burnham (note 6), vol. 4, p. 39.

13. See Michael Richman, "Edward Kemeys (1843–1907), America's First Animal Sculptor," *Fine Art Source Material Newsletter* 1 (May 1972), p. 98. Richman, pioneer researcher into the life of Edward Kemeys, made many helpful suggestions in the writing of this article.

14. Lorado Taft, *The History of American Sculpture* (New York, 1924), p. 473.

15. See Julian Hawthorne, "American Wild Animals in Art," *The Century Magazine* 28 (June 1884), pp. 213–19; and Hamlin Garland, "Edward Kemeys: A Sculptor of Frontier Life and Wild Animals," *McClure's Magazine* 5 (July 1895), pp. 120–31. Both articles are on file in the Art Institute's Ryerson and Burnham Libraries pamphlet file. The various newspaper interviews can be found in the Art Intitute Scrapbooks, Ryerson and Burnham Libraries.

16. Garland (note 15), p. 123.

17. Richman, "Edward Kemeys, Hudson Bay Wolves," *Sculpture of a City: Philadelphia's Treasures in Bronze and Stone* (New York, 1974), p. 56.

18. Richman (note 13), p. 98.

19. The Art Institute of Chicago, *Exhibitions, Catalogues, Publications*, 1879–88, vol. 2, n.p.

20. Garland (note 15), p. 127.

21. Two small bronzes and one large sculpture of a lioness and her cubs remain in the Art Institute's collections.

22. Hutchinson correspondence, Art Institute Archives.

23. Minutes of the Executive Committee meetings are on file in the Art Institute Archives.

24. This annual report was never published, but a typescript is on file in the the Art Institute Archives.

25. Burnham (note 6), vol. 4, p. 59.

26. Kemeys's lions are specifically sited at the north entrance in Johnson (note 8), vol. 3, p. 383.

27. Author's telephone interview with Michael Richman, March 10, 1988. Richman stated that full-sized models were required and were used for the Exposition and for the later casting of the Art Institute lions.

28. Interview in Art Institute Scrapbooks, Ryerson and Burnham Libraries.

29. Pamphlet file, Ryerson and Burnham Libraries. The sculptor's connection to Lathrop must have led to another major commission for him immediately after the fair, in this case not through Lathrop's sister, Mrs. Field, but his wife's brother, Owen Aldis, developer of the Marquette Building (Holabird and Roche, 1893–95). Aldis commissioned from Kemeys most of the bronze plaques of Indian chieftains and French explorers placed above the elevators on the mezzanine level of the building, as well as the panther-head door handles of the entrance. Aldis, a widower, lived for a time with the Lathrops in their home at 120 Bellevue Place (now the Fortnightly Club).

30. Pamphlet file, Ryerson and Burnham Libraries.

Bruegmann, The Art Institute Expands, pp. 57–81.

The author would like to thank Franz Schulze of Lake Forest College for his many helpful suggestions.

1. A narrow strip of land between the original building and the Illinois Central Railroad tracks, perhaps on right-of-way belonging to the railroad, also housed Art Institute buildings—notably School classrooms built in 1910, general offices constructed in 1911, and a shipping room built in 1916.

2. The story of the original agreement between the Art Institute and the Michigan Avenue property holders is sketched in Lois Wille, *Forever Open, Clear and Free: The Struggle for Chicago's Lakefront* (Chicago, 1972), p. 75. The original agreement permitting the Art Institute to be erected was contested in court since, according to one female property owner, it was only consummated by the forgery of her signature by her husband. The court overturned her claim. The injunction from building in the park has been constantly argued in the courts throughout the nineteenth and twentieth centuries, and the public's right to a green front yard was vigorously upheld by Chicago businessman Montgomery Ward in four Illinois Supreme Court cases.

3. These factors were reiterated in "Plan to Build in Grant Park Fires Old War," *Chicago Tribune*, May 15, 1929.

4. The issue of the Art Institute's air rights above the tracks crossing Grant Park was determined in 1903. The railroad has an easement, a right-of-way for railroad tracks and operations, which is limited to fifteen feet above the surface of its submerged tracks.

5. These plans are reported in clippings in the Art Institute Scrapbook in the Art Institute's Ryerson and Burnham Libraries. A story in the San Antonio, Texas, *Light*, December 4, 1927, is probably typical of others written during this period.

6. The application to the park district was reported in the *Economist*, November 5, 1927, p. 1130. Further details are contained in a story in the Chicago *Journal*, January 19, 1928, preserved in the Art Institute Scrapbook, Ryerson and Burnham Libraries.

7. Although the Art Institute successfully confirmed its right to build in *Stevens Hotel Company v. Art Institute of Chicago*, it apparently offered during the trial to enter into a voluntary agreement regulating its buildings. Among the provisions that were entered into the final decree were assurances that no new building would be higher than the existing Michigan Avenue structure, as well as a reiteration of the 400-foot limit along Michigan Avenue. See also "Plan to Build . . ." (note 3).

8. This extremely important episode in the history of the institution was amply covered in the national magazines, but, for the most extensive set of reactions, it is best to consult the collection of newspaper articles on the subject preserved in the Burnham and Ryerson Libraries clipping file. The Dallas, Texas, *News* of August 5, 1934, for example, reported that the Art Institute was jammed day after day during the entire run of the Exposition. And the Richmond, Virginia, *Times*, June 18, 1933, stated: "Never before has it been demonstrated so conclusively that America has become an art loving nation. American culture is revealed in its best light in the glory of the Chicago show."

9. According to an undated story in the Dallas, Texas, *News* preserved in the Art Institute Scrapbook, these included the Nelson Gallery in Kansas City, Missouri; the Avery Memorial in Hartford, Connecticut; the Frick Collection and the Whitney Museum of American Art in New York City; the Walters Art Gallery in Baltimore; the Lyman Allan Museum in New London, Connecticut; the Addison Gallery in Andover, Massachusetts; and new museums in Springfield and Worcester, Massachusetts; Denver; Seattle; Portland, Oregon; Columbus, Ohio; and Montclair, New Jersey.

10. The program statement has been preserved in the Edward Bennett Papers, Ryerson and Burnham Libraries, The Art Institute of Chicago.

11. It appears that all of the original competition drawings have disappeared, but photographs of the drawings exist in the Department of Photographic Services at the Art Institute. A plan and elevation of each was published in *Architectural Forum* 61 (Sept. 1934), pp. 197–200. *The Architect* (Oct. 1934), p. 210, published an elevation by Holabird and Root. The Ryerson and Burnham Libraries of the Art Institute have a portfolio containing a complete set of prints of plans, elevations, and sections by Holabird and Root, along with copies of some written materials. Preliminary sketches and a number of items collected by Holabird and Root can be found in design folder 6303 of the Holabird and Root Collection at the Chicago Historical Society; drawings for Unit A are in folder 6335. On the firm of Holabird and Root and on this competition, see the three volumes by Robert Bruegmann, *Holabird and Roche/ Holabird and Root, A Catalog of Work, 1880–1940* (forthcoming), and a two-volume set of essays on the work of the firm by Bruegmann to be published separately at a later date. Photographic prints of drawings by Walker, Grunsfeld, and Holabird and Root are in the archives of the Art Institute. The *Chicago Tribune*, July 22, 1934, published the plans of the three Chicagoans. Preliminary sketches by Paul Cret and Ralph Walker have been published in John Zukowsky, "The Art Institute of Chicago; Constructions, Concepts, and Queries," *Threshold* 3 (autumn 1985), pp. 60–74. The drawings are in the Department of Architecture.

12. Drawings for this appear in the Holabird and Root Collection of the Chicago Historical Society. The building is mentioned in "Report of the Director," *Report for the Year 1934 (Bulletin of The Art Institute of Chicago)* 29, 3 (Mar. 1935), p. 42, in an announcement of the results of the competition. Comments on the findings in the lighting experiments are found in the "Report of the Director," *Report for the Year 1935 (Bulletin of the Art Institute of Chicago)* 30, 3 (Mar. 1936), p. 33.

13. The Edward Bennett Papers (note 10) show that at least one of the competitors was upset with the results, but more because of the decision than because of charges of impropriety.

14. *Report for the Year 1934* (note 12), p. 42.

15. The story of the Ferguson Fund manipulations is well told in James L. Riedy, *Chicago Sculpture* (Chicago, 1981), pp. 8–12.

16. *Report for the Year 1935* (note 12), p. 33.

17. The new model was published in *Pencil Points* 19 (Feb. 1938), p. 77.

18. "Rehabilitation Plans," *The Art Institute of Chicago Annual Report 1954–55*, n. p.

19. According to the 1954–55 *Annual Report* (note 18), a design for a Ferguson Memorial Building had already been made in 1928.

20. The bridge across the upper level of Blackstone Hall was

removed and another floor level added. The ground floor was used to house the collection that was formerly hung on the upper floor, and a new members' lounge and the Morton Auditorium were installed on the ground level.

21. See "Art Institute Wins Fight to Build Wing," *Chicago Daily News*, June 13, 1956.

22. Museum records show that the Executive Committee approved a scale model at their meeting on September 17, 1956, and that bids went out in December 1956 and came in thirty-three percent higher than expected in January 1957. The contract with A. L. Jackson was approved on March 18, 1957.

23. On the Art Institute's money problems and resignation of director Daniel Cotton Rich, see M. W. Newman, "Art Institute World Famed—But It Has Its Troubles," *Chicago Daily News*, July 10, 1958.

24. Information on the design of the Ferguson wing was provided by John A. Holabird, Jr., in a telephone interview on February 1988.

25. Minutes of the meeting of the Committee on Buildings and Grounds, June 22, 1960. Art Institute archives.

26. Minutes of the meeting of the Committee on Buildings and Grounds, June 22 and December 19, 1960. Art Institute archives.

27. Minutes of the meeting of the Committee on Buildings and Grounds, December 19, 1960, and January 12, 1961.

28. The announcement of the new garden was made by Art Institute president William McCormick Blair at the office of Chicago mayor Richard Daley.

29. Interview with John A. Holabird, Jr., February 1988.

30. "Report of the Director of Administration," *The Art Institute of Chicago Annual Report 1959–60*, p. 4.

31. The flagpoles apparently were not selected by Holabird and Root and Burgee, but by Alfred Shaw, who was then at work on the Morton Wing.

32. The question of the fountain was discussed at the meeting of November 10, 1960, when three possibilities were suggested for a new fountain. These included a bronze fountain of lilies installed in the Rond Point of the Champs Elysées in Paris, a bronze fountain of bulrushes on display in that year's Salon d'Automne of Paris, a glass fountain designed by Max Ingrand also located at the Rond Point of the Champs Elysées. It is unclear who suggested these possibilities, but presumably the intention was to obtain a cast or copy of the fountain for Chicago. The flagpoles seem to have been included in the original garden scheme, but drawings and photographs of models in the collection of the Art Institute seem to vary on this feature. In some drawings, a piece of sculpture stands on this site.

33. McNab had a good deal of experience with museum

building prior to arriving in Chicago in June 1956. He had been involved with the building of the Lowe Gallery in Miami, Florida, the National Museum in Havana, and the Society of Four Arts Gallery in Palm Beach, Florida.

34. Minutes of the meeting of the Committee on Building and Grounds, December 9, 1959, p. 65. This committee later reported to the Executive Committee of the Trustees, who authorized a model of the new wing with the garden in front (pp. 126, 157).

35. Alfred Shaw, born in 1895, left Graham, Anderson, Probst and White in 1936 along with fellow employees Charles Murphy and Sigurd Naess to form the firm of Shaw, Naess and Murphy, later Shaw, Metz and Dolio. This firm subsequently became Shaw, Metz and Associates and, in 1961, with the joining of the firm by son Patrick Shaw, Alfred Shaw and Associates. The direction Shaw took in the postwar era is perhaps best seen at the concrete and glass building he designed for the Florsheim Shoe Co. at Canal and Adams streets, erected 1948–49, in which European modernist ideas are incorporated into a building which, in plan and general massing, still derives from the classical tradition of the 1930s.

36. On the stairway, as well as other aspects of the Morton Wing, see the collection of documents and photographs preserved in the Shaw Papers, Ryerson and Burnham Libraries, Art Institute.

37. The fight was led by the Chicago Heritage Committee, an informal group of citizens interested in the city's art, sculpture, and architecture, that had been organized in 1957 to help save Frank Lloyd Wright's Robie House in Hyde Park. Although the group did not seriously think it could halt the moving of the statue, it renewed the old issue of the use of the Ferguson Fund, saying that the Art Institute had violated the spirit of the fund by using it for buildings, and had not maintained the work that had already been commissioned. See "Art Institute Hit for Shift of Statue," *Chicago Tribune*, March 17, 1963.

38. *The Art Institute of Chicago Annual Report 1965–66*, p. 3.

39. On Kiley, see the short article in *MacMillan Encyclopedia of Architects* (1982), vol. 2, p. 565; and *Process Architecture* 33 (Oct. 1982).

40. Author's interview with Dan Kiley, February 1988.

41. The Ferguson and Morton wings have been subject to considerable criticism in the years since their completion. A typical comment on the Ferguson Wing, from a May 20, 1974, *Chicago Sun-Times* article reads: "A vast monolithic slab of masonry, flat roofed and broken only by three rows of square, unadorned windows, it might have been transported intact from the complex of capital buildings that Mussolini commissioned for Fascist Italy in the 1930s and it is the sort of imperialist structure that Albert Speer nightmared up for Adolf Hitler. In a more contemporary vein, it

looks like an IBM card on its side." But from the vantage point of the late 1980s, the building can be seen in a different light. There is a classical revival well underway among American architects, and this has had an effect on the reputation of such heavily abstracted classical buildings as John Russell Pope's National Gallery building in Washington, D.C. Although the Ferguson Wing represents a major departure from the National Gallery in trying to accommodate some of the thin, linear quality of European modernism, its astringent use of fine materials does seem to resemble the work of certain architects, such as Carlo Scarpa (1906–1978) of Italy, whose work is currently being studied by many architects and scholars. The extremely severe abstraction of classical forms resembles a good deal some of the work being done by certain contemporary European architects, such as Aldo Rossi (b. 1931).

42. An excellent summary of some of these issues can be found in an article by Chicago art critic Franz Schulze, *Daily News Panorama*, June 14 and 15, 1975.

43. *The Art Institute of Chicago Annual Report 1970–1971*, p. 4.

44. On the paintings that had been collected by Netsch by this point in time, see the catalogue for a show of selected loans from the collection of Mr. and Mrs. Walter Netsch at the University of Iowa Art Museum, *Living with Art* (Iowa City, 1971).

45. Schulze (note 42); idem., "Chicago's Art Institute Under New Management," *Art News* (Jan. 1973).

46. A discussion of the options considered by the architects is contained in an article by Nory Miller, *Daily News Panorama*, June 14 and 15, 1975.

47. Thomas Willis, "Art Institute Tells Growth Plans," *Chicago Tribune*, December 20, 1972. Dolores McCahill, "Art Institute Seeks Land in Grant Park," *Chicago Tribune*, December 20, 1972. A largely favorable review of the new building is by Franz Schulze, "Growing East: The Art Institute Expansion," *Daily News Panorama*, December 23 and 24, 1972.

48. On the plans for the Art Institute expansion and their execution, material has been incorporated from the author's interviews with Walter Netsch, Robert Hutchins, and Wayne Tjaden, all formerly with SOM.

49. Dolores McCahill, "How Uncertainty, Confusion Affected Art Institute Plan," *Chicago Tribune*, December 21, 1972.

50. Reports that the museum was negotiating the transfer of the Goodman School to the University of Illinois were disclosed, for example, in *Daily News Panorama*, June 14 and 15, 1975.

51. Donald M. Schwartz, "$46 Million Art Institute Expansion," *Chicago Sun-Times*, November 17, 1971.

52. Quoted in Rob Cuscaden, "The Art Institute of the Future," *Chicago Sun-Times*, May 20, 1974

53. In 1977, a large stained-glass window by Marc Chagall was installed in this area, eliminating the view of the facade from McKinlock Court.

54. "Judge Won't Halt Demolition of the Old Stock Exchange," *Chicago Sun-Times*, October 20, 1971; "12th Hour Drive is Made for a Chicago Landmark," *New York Times*, October 15, 1971; and "Chicago Stock Exchange Coming Down," *Preservation News*, November 1971.

55. Letter from Thomas Hoving, director of The Metropolitan Museum of Art, February 17, 1971, in the files of architect John Vinci, Chicago. An excellent essay on the merits of the Metropolitan's proposal is in Ada Louise Huxtable, "A Bad End, and A Good Idea," *New York Times*, December 26, 1971.

56. "Agree to Save Building Relics," *Chicago Tribune*, October 26, 1971; and M. W. Newman, "Owners of Stock Exchange to Save, Restore Entry Arch," *Chicago Daily News*, November 5, 1971.

57. Memos and letters by David Hanks (then an Art Institute curator) Art Institute director Charles Cunningham, city officials, the Landmarks Preservation Council, the demolition company, and lawyers representing various parties document the intense jockeying for position during the process of deciding what would be done with the Stock Exchange fragments. This correspondence is preserved in the Art Institute Archives. See Terry Shaffer, "Sullivan's art appears, disappears," *Chicago Daily News*, November 20–21, 1971. Photographer and historian Richard Nickel was killed during the demolition of the building. The best description of the salvage operation and the reconstruction of the Trading Room is found in John Vinci, *The Art Institute of Chicago: The Stock Exchange Trading Room* (Chicago, 1977).

58. Author's interviews with Walter Netsch and Robert Hutchins, both formerly of SOM, February 1988.

59. Author's interview with Walter Netsch, February 1988.

60. The problems with the placement had already been described by *New York Times* critic Ada Louise Huxtable (note 55). See also Donald Hoffmann, "Out of Time, Out of Place," *Progressive Architecture* (Nov. 1977), pp. 62–63; and Richard Christiansen, "Tearing Down and Picking Up," *Daily News Panorama*, January 1 and 2, 1972.

61. Author's interview with John Vinci, February 1988. On the recreation of the Trading Room, see Art Haydon, "Trading Room Reopens," *Chicago Sun-Times*, April 10, 1977; and M. W. Newman, *Daily News Panorama*, February 12 and 13, 1977.

62. One matter of heated debate between the architects was the degree to which the new room could duplicate the old.

Another issue concerned the matter of what work should be cut out or delayed due to insufficient funds.

63. The most cogent criticism was penned by art critic Donald Hoffmann (note 60). See also Paul Gapp, "A Glorious Fragment of Chicago's Past, Lovingly Restored," *Chicago Tribune*, April 14, 1979.

64. The designer was apparently George Dickey of that office.

65. According to Netsch, the sinking of the School garden was necessary to shield the activities of the "unconventional" students from passing motorists and pedestrians.

66. It was not published extensively in the architectural press, but see *Architectural Review*, September 1977. It was also reviewed by Nory Miller, *Daily News Panorama*, June 14 and 15, 1975.

67. The episode of the reduction in bay size was related by Wayne Tjaden, formerly of SOM, in an interview with the author, March 1988.

68. Author's interview with Robert Hutchins, February 1988.

Klawans, The Rice Building, pp. 83–98.

1. Beeby summarized his theories on the traditions of the Chicago School in an article titled "Flowering Grid," *Architectural Review* 162, 968 (Oct. 1977), pp. 223–27.

2. Quotations from James N. Wood, Thomas Beeby, Bernard Babka, and John Zukowsky derive from a series of interviews conducted with them by the author throughout 1986 and 1987.

3. *New York Times*, August 16, 1987.

4. Douglas C. McGill, *New York Times*, June 30, 1987.

5. *New York Times*, February 13, 1988.

6. Andrea Oppenheimer Dean, "Showcases for Architecture," *Architecture* 75, 1 (Jan. 1986), p. 30.

7. Douglas Davis, *Newsweek* (Feb. 23, 1987), p. 70.

8. See Carleton Knight III, "Virtuoso Performance in Stone," *Architecture* 75, 1 (Jan. 1986), pp. 40–45.

9. Joseph Giovannini, *New York Times*, October 17, 1986.

10. Robert Venturi, *Complexity and Contradiction in Architecture* (New York, 1966).

11. Vincent Scully, Jr., *Modern Architecture: The Architecture of Democracy*, rev. ed. (New York, 1974), pp. 15–16.

THE ART INSTITUTE OF CHICAGO 1988–1989

108